A History of
GOLF
Illustrated

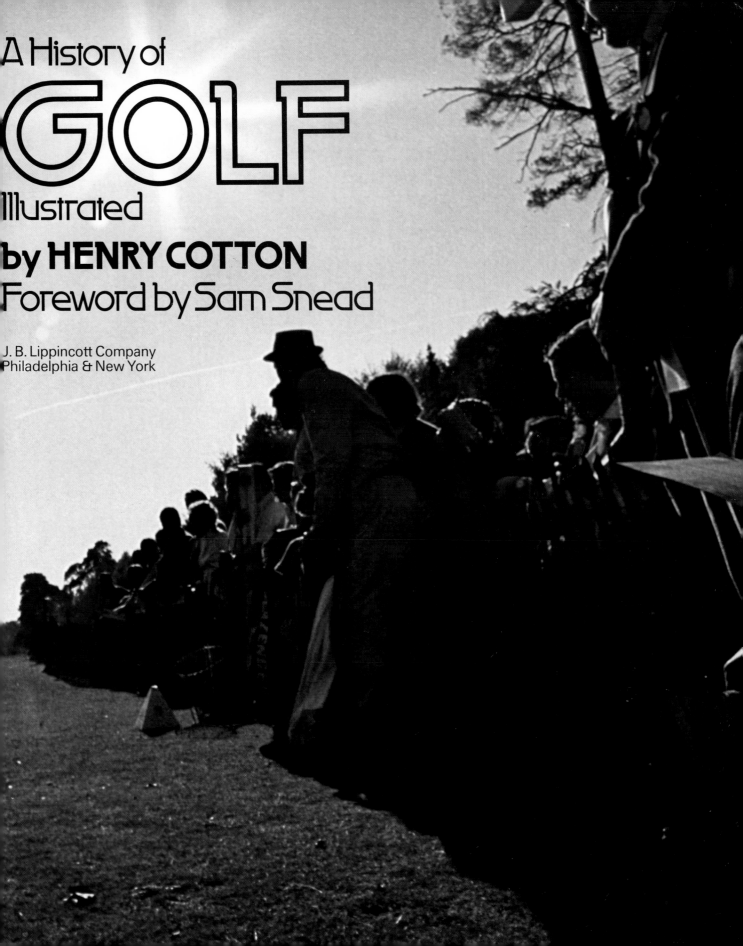

A History of
GOLF
Illustrated

by HENRY COTTON
Foreword by Sam Snead

J. B. Lippincott Company
Philadelphia & New York

Preceding page Liang Huan-Lu,
from Taiwan, symbol of the
evergrowing internationalism of
golf, drives into the evening sun
during a Piccadilly World Match-
Play Tournament at Wentworth,
England.

© Henry Cotton 1975
All rights reserved

This book was designed and
produced in Great Britain by
London Editions Limited.

Printed in Spain
D.L.: S.S. 321/75

U.S. Library of Congress Cataloging in Publication Data

Cotton, Thomas Henry, birth date
    History of golf.

    1. Golf—History.   I. Title.
GV963.C66   796.352'09   75-8530
ISBN–0-397-01092-3

Contents

Foreword by Sam Snead

I was delighted when Henry Cotton asked me to write a Foreword to his new book. Delighted because he is an old friend of mine, delighted simply to be asked, but above all delighted because Henry is one of the all-time golf greats whose services to the game on many fronts leave us deeply in his debt.

It is hard to believe that Henry has been around as a professional for over half a century. He made a good start in the south of England by winning the Kent Professional Championship for five consecutive years (1926–30), but we Americans didn't take proper notice of him until 1934. Perhaps we should have been warned in the 1929 Ryder Cup in England. Henry, partnering Ernest Whitcombe, didn't make it against Walter Hagen and Johnny Golden in the foursomes, but he put down Al Watrous in the singles 4 and 3, and it was Al who had so nearly held Bobby Jones in the Open Championship at Lytham St Anne's only three years before, playing that fantastic third round of 69.

And then in 1934 . . . For ten years Britain had been unable to break American domination in her Open. Henry did it by five whole strokes over Bobby Locke's partner Sid Brews. And then he won it again in 1937, *and* again in 1948, and in that span of fourteen years, much of them spent in war service, he managed to win three British PGA championships and the Belgian, Italian, German, Czech and French Open titles, making him without doubt the greatest British professional since Vardon.

But Henry's more than a fine practitioner. 'Concentration Henry', as Walter Hagen dubbed him, has been described as remote. He is not remote. He loves life and people, animals and flowers, but he thinks, and he thinks and cares very deeply about golf. As a teacher and writer he has never insisted on a style or a method as being the only one. He's experimented with most of them himself. But for longer than one cares to remember he has advocated, with admirable independence, that 'open to shut' is quite as good, and easier, than 'shut to open' or 'square to square', and in the face of years of watching top professionals winning the major tournaments with styles quite unlike his own, he has advocated what, after all, Vardon, Braid and Taylor used and won with seventy years ago – and I have used all my golfing life.

And now? Arnold Palmer, Gary Player and Jack Nicklaus are back to 'open to shut' and by one of those strange ironies, Henry, retired from tournament golf, is besieged with letters from professionals and amateurs all over the world begging for help and advice. They have only to go to Penina in the Algarve in Portugal and I know he will be only too pleased to spend time helping them.

Penina Golf Course is a sort of tangible monument to Henry and to another side of him. This most beautiful course, with its luxury hotel, was only built about ten years ago on what had formerly been a rice field. It is now one of the finest courses in Europe, laid out and looked after by Henry. Stands of eucalyptus have already topped 70 feet so that he has been able to see his own plans grow and mature in a way that must be as satisfying to him as Augusta was to Bobby Jones. It's a very tough course indeed of 6889 yards, going up to 7480 for championship length, with an unusual par 35 out, 38 in, but it perfectly reflects Henry's beliefs. The hazards, which include natural water as well as the bunkers, trees and rough, are strategic, not always penal, but with skill it is tameable. Valentin Barrios has subdued it in tournament with a round of 66 and Neil Coles, the British professional, came close to equalling this record with a 68 in the 1974 Portuguese Open.

Henry has designed many courses. He believes that golf is for enjoyment and that enjoyment embraces skill. He sees no point in penalizing a player for a well-hit shot or for wet-nursing a player with non-existent roughs if he's not prepared to play within his abilities. He does not have prejudices. On the vexed and tiresome question of 'the ball', though he would be happy to see a standardized size and weight, he is honest enough to say, 'The large ball (1.62oz $\times$ 1.68in.) has contributed as much to the improvement in the general standard of American golf as has the steel shaft in the world at large.' I would like to say that Henry has contributed as much to the wellbeing of golf as has anyone living, and I hope that this beautifully illustrated book with Henry's invaluable advice and knowledge of the game will be on every golfer's bookshelf – or by his bed.

I will only add that Henry is the greatest European golfer I have ever seen and played with or against.

Sam Snead
White Sulphur Springs, 1975

When I started putting together the material for this book, I did not intend merely to assemble the historic facts about how golf began but to present a story of golf from its early days, including the actual playing of the game as I see it. I am afraid that millions of new players, amateurs and professionals, get hold of some golf clubs and balls and just begin to play golf, without fully realizing that they have become part of one of the greatest sporting brotherhoods in the world and have an obligation to know something of the origins of golf and of the players who have been responsible for the early and more recent developments in the game. Golf certainly has the largest number of active participants of any game played with a ball and a stick and the numbers increase daily throughout the world. This is the ninth book I have written and it will be the first to be published in languages other than English, so I am particularly proud to know that its distribution will cover the globe and serve to bring to many other nations the traditions of the game they are beginning to love and enjoy.

Having now been a golf professional for over fifty years, and having earned my living from the game as club professional, champion, golf architect, lecturer on the sport, variety star with my own golf act, author and regular contributor to golf magazines and newspapers since 1931, golf club designer and promoter, it can be imagined that I know the game 'inside out'.

I have not tried to find the best players ever, because no golfer can ever be really other than the best in his generation, with golf courses, rules and equipment changing all the time – but I hope this book will amuse and interest millions of golfers old and new.

Henry Cotton
Penina, January 1975

1 The Origins and Early Days

GOLF TODAY is such a fine game to play and watch that you might well wonder why we should need, however briefly, to examine its obscure beginnings in the Middle Ages. Well, it is always useful to begin at the beginning, and when the beginning, like so much else in golf, is a matter of permanent and delightful controversy among its devotees, why not have a few facts at one's fingertips?

Much has been written about the earliest days, and new documents supporting one argument or another regularly turn up in dusty archives. It seems, however, that golf almost certainly originated in Scotland – that is, the game as we know it. Various other ball games played all over Europe have been advanced as ancestors, but none of them appear to have had that combination of peculiarities which distinguish golf from other sports. Two essential characteristics set golf apart: it combines both the ability to hit the ball long distances and the more intimate skill of putting it into a very small target, the hole; it also does not allow one player to interfere with the other's game (except in the case of the now defunct stymie). The continental games seem only to have had superficial resemblances.

The word 'golf' is connected with the German word *kolb*, a club, and confusion has arisen over various French and Low Countries games with somewhat similar names, especially *chole* and *kolven*, but their relevance to our subject is doubtful, and I shall leave the reader to consult the authorities, especially Robert Browning in *A History of Golf: The Royal and Ancient Game* (1955).

Early references to the game are sparse. There is a recorded sale of a golf ball (for 10 Scottish shillings) in 1452. The Fourteenth Parliament of James II of Scotland on 6 March 1457 enacted a decree that 'fut ball and golfe must be utterly cryit dune'. This suggests that the two games had become so popular that they were luring men away from the archery practice essential for the defence of their country against England. But the stubborn Scots clearly took little notice, for

This club-swinging stained-glass figure is in the great east window of Gloucester Cathedral, England. The head is missing. The window was built 1340-50, and if this really is a depiction of a golfer it is much the earliest pictorial representation known

Left This early manuscript drawing shows a game which could well have been golf. The ball is large and possibly made of boxwood, while the clubs appear curved like hockey sticks. 14th century

Right Young Dutch boy, with iron and feathery ball. The club, if held upright, would reach to his chin, which suggests that strokes were long and sweeping. The stitching on the ball can be clearly seen. 17th century

in 1491 James IV's Parliament decreed: 'It is statute and ordained that in na place of the Realme there be used Fute-ball, Golf, or uther sik unprofittable sportis' contrary to 'the common good of the Realme and defense thereof'. This time the law not only fixed a fine and jail for those caught at the game but also for those on whose land the game was being played. But it must have been about this time that James himself, who is supposed to have insisted that golf was a ridiculous sport with no strength or skill, fell under its magic. The Lord High Treasurer's accounts of 1502 show the following entry:

Item: The xxi day of September, to the bowar of Sanct Johnestown for clubbs.
xiiijs.

and in 1504:

The third day of Februar, to the King to play at the Golf with the Erle of Bothuile, iij French crowns. sumena, xlijs.
For Golf Clubbis and Ballis to the King that he playit with. lxs.

Some have said that when King James had his game with the Earl of Bothwell he was breaking his own law. But in fact the law was by then redundant, for in February 1502, in Glasgow Cathedral, the king had signed a treaty of perpetual peace with England and had announced his forthcoming marriage to Princess Margaret, the daughter of Henry VII of England. The wedding took place at Holyrood Palace in August 1503.

This connubial alliance may have brought golf into brief popularity in England, for Catherine of Aragon, Henry VIII's wife number one, wrote in 1513 to Cardinal Wolsey: 'And all his [Henry VIII's] subjects be very glad, Master Almoner, I thank God, to be busy with the golf, for they take it for pastime.' Tragically, within a month, the battle of Flodden had been fought and James IV and the flower of his nobility were slain. Scotland and England were at war.

Golf, however, flourished in Scotland and with football became the joint national sport, and a royal sport. James V played frequently at Gosford, in East Lothian, where he set up a private links, and his tragic daughter, Mary Queen of Scots, was charged with being seen 'playing golf and pall-mall in the fields beside Seton' shortly after the murder of her husband, Lord Darnley. Mary, incidentally, had learned the game at an early age and had continued to play in France, where she was later schooled. Students carried her clubs for her and she called them 'cadets'. This is probably the origin of the word caddie.

The Scottish game was played on 'links', a name which today has tended to become associated with the natural courses by the sea. But there is no good reason for restricting the term, for it seems that 'links' meant much the same as the southern English 'downs', with

Young Dutch Kolfer by Albert Cuyp (1650). This well-dressed boy is quite clearly playing a feathery with an iron at a seaside links

Right Print after a painting by Adriaen van de Velde (*c.* 1668). The player is aiming for a post, just visible over his left shoulder
Below right A member of the Society of Golfers at Blackheath, near London, dressed in the club finery. Even the caddie is smartly attired. The complement of clubs appears to be five woods and three irons. 18th century

no specific connection either with the sea or the game of golf. But links or no links, when James VI of Scotland ascended the throne of England as James I, in 1603, he brought the game into a favour in England from which it has never withdrawn.

Golf continued through the seventeenth century as a game for all classes. Matches were played for wagers, sometimes on private courses, sometimes on open land, but there were no official rules and the number of holes varied according to the extent of the land over which the games were played. Only in the eighteenth century did any real shape come into the game.

However, golf courses, or at least the places where the game was played, were becoming more formal. Gosford has already been mentioned. Mary Queen of Scots also played at St Andrews. In 1608 a 7-hole course was laid out at Blackheath, near London, apparently for the diversion of some of James I's Scottish courtiers, who had become disenchanted with staghunting and wished to pursue their native sport. They played their

TO THE SOCIETY OF GOFFERS AT BLACKHEATH

15

game with hockey-stick-shaped clubs and feather balls. In the year of his accession to the English throne, James I appointed William Mayne golf-club maker and in 1618 a student at St Andrews University, James Melvill, was appointed golf-ball maker on a twenty-one-year lease and an embargo was placed on balls being imported from Holland. This apparently was to save money being sent out of the country. In the same year the king lifted the ban on Sunday golf (imposed in Edinburgh in 1592), provided that players attend divine service first. The replacement of the bow and arrow by firearms and the consequent demise of the need for archery practice undoubtedly hastened royal approval of the game. It also released many bowyers from their time-old craft, and many of them eagerly set about making golf clubs, where their skills could be perfectly utilized.

Throughout the seventeenth century royal enthusiasm promoted the game's growth. Charles I was playing on the links at Leith, near Edinburgh, when news came of the Irish Rebellion. He also used to play during his confinement at Newcastle. James II played throughout his exile and was the creator of the first international match, between England and Scotland. This came about because two English noblemen claimed that England not Scotland was the home of golf (probably basing their imputation on the early origins of Blackheath). To prove Scotland's true claim, the Duke of York, later James II, challenged the two Englishmen to a foursome against himself and a Scotsman of his choice. After a thorough search for an able golfer the Duke's choice fell on a cobbler, John Patersone, and largely through the cobbler's prowess the Scottish pair thoroughly trounced

Above This frost scene by A. van der Neer shows how popular the game must have been on the Continent in the 17th century
Right It is difficult to understand how so long a club could have been controlled with so light a grip in this 18th-century drawing by J. Andriessen

Golf in Victorian times could be
either a gentlemanly sport, as
here, or a rather more rumbustious
game, as the next illustration
shows

the Englishmen and settled the rival claims for once and all – or almost. Patersone was awarded a considerable bonus and a coat of arms.

We can visualize those early links. They were narrow strips of land winding naturally through the contours of dune or hill. Though there were no written rules, it seems that a code of conduct was strictly adhered to. It was proper to wear a jacket when playing and, because the same holes were used for going out and coming in, and the greens, such as they were, were used both as tees and for putting, protocol demanded that incoming players were to be given priority and that balls should be teed at a reasonable distance from the hole. (In fact it would appear from the earliest written rules that the distance was to be no more than one club's length.)

The balls were made of feather and leather ('featheries'). These had been used from the earliest days of the game (though beech, boxwood, even ivory or iron, were also used). In fact the Romans had played a game called *paganica* with curved sticks and featheries, and although the Roman balls were larger than golf balls their manufacture was almost identical. Featheries were slow to make and extremely expensive. Tanned leather, usually bullhide, or sometimes horsehide, was cut to make 2-, 3- or 4-lobe-shaped strips which were then soaked in a solution of alum to soften them. After stitching the lobes together, the ballmaker turned this cover inside out, leaving a small quarter-inch hole unstitched. Through this aperture he would stuff a whole hatful of boiled goose feathers, using a kind of awl (the 'brogue') set at right angles in a piece of wood which he pressed against his chest to give more pressure. To keep the ball spherical, he used a leather cup (the 'socket') as a rough mould. After the hole had been stitched up, the balls were left to dry out and the swelling of the feathers and the contraction of the leather produced a hard, solid sphere. This was then waterproofed by rubbing with oil, and scoured with chalk to make it more visible.

Doubtless James Melvill's ballmaking monopoly was a highly profitable one. We do not know who took over from him, but certainly in 1642 Aberdeen was prepared to issue a licence to one John Dickson. The art of ballmaking, with balls costing as much as 2s 6d each, was jealously guarded, as were the balls themselves. In 1637 a boy was hanged for stealing golf balls. Inhuman though this seems, the ballmakers themselves were prone to slow and early deaths. Accumulated feather dust in the lungs and the pressure of the 'brogue' on the craftsmen's chests caused havoc with respiratory systems. And though the prices were high, only four or five balls a day could be made by one man.

By the nineteenth century there were many famous families of ballmakers – the Robertsons, Hutchisons, Auchterlonies and Forgans were among the best known. Allan Robertson, for instance, who died in 1859 at the age of forty-four, was producing, in partnership with Tom Morris, between 1000 and 2500 balls a year, but even this sort of output could not provide the cheap balls that the vast majority of golfers could afford. The Gourlays of Leith (later of Musselburgh) were generally accepted as the finest makers, but their products could cost as much as four or five shillings (about one dollar).

Clubs, like balls, changed very little until the middle of the nineteenth century. The early evidence is scarce, but we can see in the work of Dutch and Flemish painters of the seventeenth century that club shapes were almost identical to those depicted in paintings by English artists of the eighteenth and early nineteenth centuries. The oldest known set of clubs (probably early seventeenth-century) can be seen in the clubhouse at Troon, on the west coast of Scotland. They are inordinately long woods with narrow heads, and players must have had to adopt an extremely flat swing even to manipulate them. Woods were probably the play clubs and were certainly lofted to different degrees – long spoon, mid-spoon, short spoon and baffing spoon – much as are modern clubs. Irons at the time were

It looks as though a bet may well have been put on this putt. Concentration was clearly difficult, and sheep were natural hazards apparently only used to get out of trouble from difficult lies such as ditches and ruts.

These deep-bladed irons were quite unsuitable for the delicate leather skins of the featheries and it was not until the coming of the gutta-percha ball in 1848 that the potential of irons for approach shots was fully realized. Allan Robertson, who pioneered the use of irons for approach shots, also substituted the iron putting cleek for the wooden putter on the greens, for the 'gutty' could be stroked towards the hole with an iron in a way very different from the featheries' bouncing effect. And so the shape and use of clubs moved towards today's standards. Young Tom Morris introduced the niblick (approximately no. 9 iron), which facilitated the short pitch shot with a large degree of backspin; J. H. Taylor (the first great English-born professional) perfected play with the mashie (no. 5 iron), which he used with a short swing and a firm punching stroke, quite unlike the accepted long sweeping swing of the day; and later, as we shall see, the wedge and steel-shafted clubs came in.

Of course, there is another type of golf club, and perhaps more argument has surrounded the formation of clubs and clubhouses than about any other golfing topic. Part of the confusion undoubtedly stems from the early use of the word 'club'. Until the mid-eighteenth century games had been played over links without any rules laid down, without any organized association and with greenkeepers employed on an *ad hoc* basis. When in 1744 'several Gentlemen of Honour, skilfull in the ancient and healthfull exercise of Golf' petitioned the City of Edinburgh to provide a Silver Club for an annual competition on the links of Leith, one can accept the year as the inception of the Company of Gentlemen Golfers, now the Honourable Company of Edinburgh Golfers, for the presentation of a trophy has been a concomitant of the formation of practically every eighteenth-century golf club. If this can be accepted, it is fair to acclaim the Honourable Company as the oldest of all golf clubs. St

Andrews followed the Leith example ten years later, in 1754. The annual winners of these competitions were designated Captains of Golf and the current holder of the title became the referee in any dispute which might arise. The early tournaments for the Silver Club had been open to all-comers, but as it happened only a few local players from Leith and St Andrews competed. In 1764, therefore, the Captains of Golf at Leith sought authority from the City of Edinburgh to 'admit such Noblemen and Gentlemen as they approve to be Members of the Company of Golfers' and to allow only these members to do battle for the Silver Club. This move, with its conditions for membership, is to some modern thinking a better date for the formation of the Club.

The Honourable Company has at its present club at Muirfield a paper of a code of thirteen articles and rules drawn up in 1744. The early St Andrews code of 1754 was almost identical and was certainly copied from the Leith one. Among other stipulations, the ball was to be teed within a club's length of the hole, the player whose ball lay further from the hole played first, and the ball was not to be changed after being struck off the tee. There were also stipulations about penalty strokes and hazards. All in all it was a neat and simple conduct of play, and any disputes which lay outside its thirteen paragraphs could be settled by the Captain.

The Company used the links at Leith as its home until the 1820s, but as housing sprung up it became more and more unsatisfactory and eventually the Company was wound up and sold its possessions. In 1836 the Company was re-formed and moved to Musselburgh, where it happily stayed until 1891, when finding perfect golfing country near Gullane it constructed the great links of Muirfield, where it remains.

The Society of St Andrews Golfers used to meet in the Black Bull Tavern or at Bailie Glass's, but when William IV granted it the resounding title of Royal and Ancient in 1834 and became its patron it gained even greater

Above A whole hatful of feathers, like this, was stuffed into the leather casing of a feathery ball *Right* Four clubs from the St Andrews golf museum. Many such eccentric clubs have been banned over the years. All were invented with some clever idea in mind for improving play. The putter in the centre even has a viewfinder to help the player on his line of play

respectability and in 1835 used the new Union Club as its regular headquarters. As the century wore on, St Andrews became the accepted home of the game, as it still unquestionably is today.

Other clubs came into existence in the eighteenth century: Musselburgh 1774, the Edinburgh Burgess Golfing Society 1773, the Bruntsfield Links Golf Club 1787, the Glasgow Club 1787. But the nineteenth century was when the great majority of famous clubs were inaugurated, particularly in the last three decades.

Though the membership was strictly limited in the early clubs, the games themselves were played over public courses. However, the club atmosphere prevailed strongly on the links and the members proudly wore extravagant uniforms – and indeed were fined if they omitted to do so. Most uniforms boasted scarlet jackets, though Glasgow wore grey, and their use continued well into the nineteenth century, with a few clubs clinging on to the custom into the present century. Extravagance reached a peak with the Burgess Society whose members in 1837 were obliged to wear 'a dress coat, colour dark claret, with black velvet collar, double-breasted and lined in the skirts with white silk or satin, prominent buttons on cuffs of coat and also on the flaps, dress vest colour primrose with smaller buttons to correspond with those on the coat'. This peacock equipment was only used for gala occasions, but there are plenty of records of the dining and wining which regularly took place on such occasions, and the North Berwick Club, in particular, appears to have been as much a social as a golf club and even allowed lady guests to lunch.

The first club formed outside Scotland was the Honourable Company of Golfers in 1787 at Blackheath, near London, where golf had been played since 1608, and by the 1850s about thirty-five clubs had been started in the British Isles. The first continental society was founded at Pau in France in 1856. The Duke of Wellington's Scottish soldiers who had halted here on the long march home from the Peninsular War remembered this bit of ideal golfing country and some returned to live and build a golf course, but the spread of golf abroad belongs to later chapters. The 1840s saw the end of the featheries and golf entered the second phase of its development and growth.

THE DAY OF THE FEATHERY was passing. Allan Robertson, a leading ball-maker at St Andrews, was by 1844 turning out 2456 a year, and helping him was his protégé 'Old' Tom Morris. But with the advent of the gutta-percha ball and Old Tom's adoption of this innovation, the two had a bitter row and Old Tom left Robertson, not to return until his tutor died in 1859. The accepted story about the introduction of the gutty was that the material – a juice produced by various trees of the family Sapotaceae, which coagulates on exposure to air – had been used to pack a statue of Vishnu sent from India. Whoever first realized its potentialities as a substitute for the expensive, poor-wearing feathery, its exploitation is credited to the Reverend Dr Robert Adams Paterson in 1845. The first balls appeared under the name 'Paterson's Patent'. From a rod of gutta-percha about 1½in. diameter, slices were taken off and softened in warm water and then simply moulded into globes. The first balls were smooth, though some had lines scratched to imitate the stitching of the featheries, but it was soon realized that older balls with cut marks on them from mishits flew better than new ones and soon new balls were being intentionally cut with a tool. Later, dimpling with the narrow end of a hammer prevented the balls from ducking in flight, as happened when they were completely smooth, and some form of dimpling has been used ever since on golf balls. The balls were about 1.68in. diameter, but their weights differed and patrons could select whatever weight they wished. The finest of these early balls were made by Old Tom Morris, Forgan and the Auchterlonies and had brand names such as 'Eureka', 'Henley', 'OK', 'A1', 'Agrippa', 'White Brand', and so on. Another ball, the 'Eclipse', was produced during this period, made of secret ingredients but thought to contain india rubber and a cork filling. Its popularity was waning by the 1890s.

The new ball also had an effect on the manufacture of clubs. Being harder, it necessitated stronger and more resilient clubs,

Right 'Quiet, please', on the 1st tee as Old Tom Morris (extreme left) and Allan Robertson (centre with a cluster of clubs under his arms) watch captain Hay Wemyss drive off. Old Tom won the British Open Championship four times, Robertson never. Yet Robertson set the fashion of using iron clubs from the fairway. The two played many foursome matches as partners and were said never to have been beaten
Below Old Tom Morris in his later days. His name is commemorated on the Old Course at St Andrews by the Tom Morris hole, the 18th
Below right The first refreshment bar? Auld Daw, a famous St Andrews character, is seen serving Old Tom Morris with a glass of milk at the 9th hole, about 1875

Far left An elegant photograph of Young Tom Morris, proudly wearing the (British) Open Championship belt that was awarded to the winner in those days. By winning it for three years in succession (1868-70) he was allowed to keep it. The Championship then went into abeyance for one year, being revived in 1872 on the presentation of a cup
Left Young Tom Morris's monument at St Andrews. The floral tribute was laid by the 1938 US Walker Cup team. Though he looks calm enough here, he was extremely energetic on the course, and it is said that so furiously would he waggle his clubs that the shafts sometimes broke!

and because it was less easily damaged, iron clubs were made in far greater numbers. Woods became squatter, and apple, pear and beech replaced the unyielding thorn for the club heads, and leather faces were fitted to the hitting area of the woods, to prevent excessive wear.

Allan Robertson, who was semi-official professional at St Andrews, was a magnificent short game player, but unhappily his argument with Old Tom meant that the two never met in single combat in a challenge match. However, whatever the result of such a match might have been, Robertson's record-breaking 79 over the Old Course with a feathery shows that he was a remarkable player. There were frequent challenge matches in those days and some of the finest took place between combinations of Allan Robertson (St Andrews), Tom Morris (Prestwick), Willie and Jamie Dunn (Blackheath) and Willie Park (Musselburgh). The finest match was played in 1849 over North Berwick, St Andrews and Musselburgh, when Robertson and Morris defeated the Dunns by a single hole and won the £400 prize contributed by club members.

The 1850s, with the gutty firmly established, proved to be the beginning of the growth of the modern game. William IV had conferred the 'Royal' title on St Andrews, and in 1854 the clubhouse was completed and formally assumed its full title – The Royal and Ancient Golf Club of St Andrews becoming the Mecca of golf and its central inspiration.

There was little difference in those days in Scotland between amateur and professional. The amateurs, 'gentlemen golfers', were the financial sponsors of organized golf, but all played together in fiercely contested matches over the rough courses, and much money was laid on the side for bets.

All through the 1850s golf clubs were being formed – and in 1856, Pau in France was inaugurated, the first golf club on the Continent. The first club championship match was played at St Andrews in 1857 and drew eleven clubs into the competition. Blackheath

Below An artist's impression of the golf links at Pau, in France, the earliest Continental course, 1884. It was founded in 1856 by the Duke of Hamilton, and patronized by the British who wintered at the base of the Pyrenees

won. In 1858 Allan Robertson played his record-breaking round at St Andrews, and in the same year W. R. Chambers became the world's first amateur champion in the first Grand National Amateur championship played at St Andrews.

Then in 1860 the first British Open ('The Open') was played. It was only for professionals and there were eight entries. It was played over three rounds of the 12-hole Prestwick course, with a fine Morocco belt studded with silver ornaments as the first prize. Willie Park won, beating Old Tom Morris by 2 strokes. But Tom Morris had his revenge in the two successive years over Willie Park until Willie Park retrieved his title in 1863, the first year that money prizes had been presented for the second, third and fourth place finishers. (The prizes were £5, £3 and £2.) Tom Morris went on to win twice again, in 1864 and 1867. All the early Opens were held at Prestwick and it was not until 1873 that the venues began to alternate. The second (1861) Open was competed for by both professionals and amateurs, but the

battle of the Belt, which was to be presented *in perpetuo* after three consecutive victories, did not end until 1870, when Young Tom Morris won for the third successive time. (In 1871 no Open was held.) He won again in 1872.

'Young' Tom Morris, the old man's son, was a very great golfer. He attracted the crowds when he was only thirteen and he won his first British Open when he was just eighteen. In that year, 1868, he took 157 for the 36 holes, 13 better than his father's previous year's total; but to be fair, Old Tom Morris, who was runner-up, was home with a fine score of 158. By 1870 Young Tom had shot 149. He has been compared with Arnold Palmer – an aggressive hitter who could get into trouble and out of it without difficulty.

The Scottish enthusiasm was catching on fast in England and in 1864 the Royal North Devon and Westward Ho! clubs were started by a Scottish general, to be followed by other famous English clubs – Wimbledon (1865), Hoylake (the Royal Liverpool Golf Club) (1869) and the Royal St George's, Sandwich

Above left Get yourself out of that! A sympathetic audience watch a competitor struggle to get his ball out of a St Andrews bunker, c. 1865
Above A familiar sight to those who have played golf on the banks of Scotland's Firth of Forth —North Berwick from Point Garry. This is a typical seaside links, with dunes and natural sand traps

(1887). Clubs were also formed in Wales and Ireland. In 1870 the Adelaide Golf Club was formed in Australia, followed three years later by one in Montreal. The Royal Montreal Golf Club had a fifteen-year start on the first United States Club. Young Tom Morris's death in 1875 at the age of twenty-four deprived golf of one whom some think may have been its greatest practitioner.

The Open alternated between three Scottish clubs, Prestwick, Musselburgh and St Andrews, until 1891, and two Scottish players matched Young Tom Morris's success in winning for three consecutive years – Jamie Anderson of St Andrew's (1877–9) and Bob Ferguson of Musselburgh (1880–2), but Scotland at last succumbed to English pressure when the amateur John Ball, of Hoylake, Cheshire, took the title in 1890. By 1892 Muirfield (the Honourable Company of Edinburgh Golfers) had been added to the circuit and Musselburgh dropped out. 1892 was also the year when English dominance began to show it had really arrived, for Harold Hilton won the Open at Muirfield in a match which had been extended for the first time to 72 holes. From this point until World War I, golf was dominated by the Great Triumvirate

Above A sketch of a golf match (1870) at Royal Blackheath, perhaps the oldest club in England. Claims to its foundation in 1608 are unsubstantiated, but the club does possess a silver club bearing the inscription: 'August 16, 1766 a gift of Mr Henry Foot to the Honourable Company of Goffers at Blackheath'
Right Possibly the first golf photograph taken in America. Left to right (excluding the boys) are Harry Holbrook, A. Kinnan, John B. Upham and John Reid on the cow pasture at Yonkers, New York, which was to become the St Andrews course

Charles Blair Macdonald (1856-1932) who in 1895 became the first US Amateur champion, beating Charles E. Sands in the 36-hole final by 12 and 11. Subsequently Macdonald designed the National Links on Long Island which has many British characteristics. He also became a founder member of the United States Golf Association

Right A. J. Balfour, a future British prime minister, as seen by an artist, driving off from the 1st tee at St Andrews, Scotland, 1894, the custom of all incoming Captains of the Royal and Ancient. The caddie who collects the ball is to this day rewarded with a gold sovereign
Far right Golfers apparently had their ailments even in the late 1800s

ELLIMANS UNIVERSAL EMBROCATION 1/1½

"IT I WILL HAVE OR I WILL HAVE NONE"

Prepared only by Elliman Sons & Co Slough

FOR STIFFNESS ❧ ACHES SPRAINS ❧ BRUISES

– J. H. Taylor (England), James Braid (Scotland) and Harry Vardon (Channel Islands).

But in the United States much had happened. John G. Reid, like so many other subsequent American players, had been born in Scotland – Dunfermline to be precise. He is considered the 'father of American golf', though in fact there had been 'golf clubs' in the States since at least 1795, when a notice in the Charleston, South Carolina, *City Gazette* proclaimed the anniversary party of the Golf Club; but it seems that these early 'golf clubs' were purely for social functions and there is no evidence that the game itself was ever played. John Reid had made a fair amount of money in J. L. Mott Iron Works, Mott Haven, and by 1880 he was indulging his natural ability at sports by shooting and playing tennis in his spare time. This sporting instinct turned his thoughts to the game which was so amazingly popular in his home country, and when a close friend, Robert Lockhart,

happened to be travelling on business to Britain in 1887, Reid suggested he buy clubs and balls there. And so Lockhart, taking his commission seriously, journeyed up to St Andrews and from the shop of Old Tom Morris himself he bought a driver, brassie and spoon, and a cleek, sand-iron and putter, plus a couple of dozen gutta-percha balls.

On 22 February 1888, John Reid invited some of his friends along, and over three makeshift holes of about 100 yards each on his old cow pasture at Yonkers, Westchester County, New York, he played the historic first game of golf in the States, against John B. Upham. The game was so successful that more clubs were ordered and in the following April they decided to move to more spacious grounds where they laid out six holes over the rough pasture. The usual participants – Reid, Upham, Harry Holbrook, Kingman H. Putnam and Henry Tallmadge – enjoyed themselves all summer over the six holes with their bumpy twelve-foot greens, and on

14 November 1888 after dinner at John Reid's house the St Andrew's Golf Club was founded. Robert Lockhart was elected the first active member. By March 1889 there were thirteen members, but when the City of Yonkers planned to drive a road straight through the course its members upped clubs and pitched their greens a quarter of a mile away in a 34-acre apple orchard. A fine apple tree which shaded the home green became their 19th hole and the Yonkers golfers were nicknamed 'The Apple Tree Gang'.

Though popular enough by the time the St Andrews Golf Club was founded, it is interesting to realize just how few courses there were scattered through the world in 1888. Scotland topped the list with seventy-three and England boasted fifty-two, but there were only twenty-five others, and eight of those were in the British Isles. But after 1888 American clubs began to proliferate. Tuxedo Golf Club, Tuxedo Park, New York followed in 1889 and by 1894 there were forty-two clubs, and some forty more courses made their appearance in the States in the next year. St Andrews, Yonkers, was having its troubles. The oldest American golf course was too small for the number of its keen members, and other courses, such as Newport, RI, (9 holes) and Shinnecock Hills, Long Island, with seventy-five members and a magnificent clubhouse, made the Apple Tree Gang's facilities seem inadequate. Chicago had two 18-hole courses and after a sad amount of internal wrangling St Andrews moved to Grey Oaks, three miles away, in May 1894. A farmhouse there became the clubhouse and with grey gaiters, grey knickers, plaid stockings, blue-checked waistcoats, winged collars, blue checked caps, and the traditional red coats with brass buttons, the members rapidly multiplied. The first US Amateur was played at Grey Oaks in 1894 and the club was also behind the formation of the United States Golf Association. But in 1897 the club moved again, for the fourth and last time, to Mt Hope, and there with an 18-hole course it has stayed.

Shinnecock Hills will always be regarded as the first 'proper' course in America. Whereas the game had been played over rough fields with huge enjoyment, at Shinnecock, at the eastern end of Long Island, a magnificent 12-hole course was laid out by Willie Dunn, the Scottish course architect and professional. Dunn had been appointed in 1889 by W. K. Vanderbilt, Edward S. Mead and Duncan Cryder, while he was laying out the 18-hole course at Biarritz. Shinnecock Hills was opened in June 1891, and with forty-four members buying from 1 to 10 shares at $100 each, it became the first incorporated golf club in the country. Theodore Havemeyer, the 'Sugar King', also provided a boost for the game with his Brenton's Point, Newport course (1890) – this was in real millionaires' country, with J. J. Astor, Cornelius Vanderbilt and Oliver Belmont among its local patrons.

It is interesting that in a time when women were hardly thought of as pioneers of sport, Miss Florence Boit, who had learnt the game at Pau, introduced it to her uncle, Arthur Hunnewell, who laid out a pitch-and-putt course over his lawns and the lawns of two neighbours. One devotee, Laurence Curtis, attracted to the game at the Hunnewells, recommended that The Country Club, Brookline, should include the game among its facilities and consequently a 6-hole course was laid out.

Most of these early courses had been in the East and they had been short courses of 6, 9 or 12 holes, but in 1893 Chicago, flamboyantly asserting the West's interest in golf, built the first 18-hole course in the United States. The driving force was a remarkable man, Charles Blair Macdonald, who was in the forefront of every dispute in the American game until he died in 1928. He was rich, domineering, articulate and stubborn. He was also a fine amateur, whose schooling in his late teens at St Andrews in Scotland made him a rigorous defender of the Royal and Ancient and all it stood for. Not for him a game that changed its rules as it developed in its new country; he wanted to emulate as nearly as possible the

One of the early examples showing that golf was not a game confined to Europe. The scene is Secunderabad, Madras, the largest military station at the time in India

spirit, layout and traditions of the great British courses. He was always in the centre of controversy and in the course of his life he made many enemies, but gained many staunch friends.

After architecting a miniature course of 7 holes at Lake Forest (no hole exceeded 250 yards), he and his friends at the Chicago Club raised the money for a 9-hole course at Belmont which was extended to 18 holes in 1893, and the next year they bought a 200-acre farm at Wheaton for $28,000, which C. B. Macdonald transformed into a championship course. Soon Chicago was swept by the golf craze and by 1900 it sported twenty-six golf clubs, but the Chicago Golf Club remained the premier for many years and has seen more major championships than any other course in America.

Meanwhile, all round the world, and especially in the British Empire, golf flourished and began to take on all the trappings of the modern game. John Ball Jr had won both the British Open and Amateur in 1890; Ireland had held its first amateur championship at Portrush in 1892, and in the same year Harold H. Hilton won the British Open at Muirfield. Gate money was charged for an exhibition match, also in 1892, between Jack White and Douglas Rolland at Chesterfield, in the English Midlands. In 1893 the Ladies Golf Union was formed in Britain and Lady Margaret Scott won the first British Ladies Championship at Lytham and St Annes.

Back in the States, C. B. Macdonald was as so often fighting a lone battle. In 1894 Newport Golf Club had arranged a match for golfers from all clubs to compete on their newly extended Rocky Farm course. One of the features of the course was stone walls that straddled some of the fairways. These were thought by some to be splendid hazards. Not so Macdonald. When he lost by one stroke to W. G. Lawrence from Newport, partly as a result of a 2-stroke penalty when his ball rolled under one of those walls, he declined to accept Lawrence's victory, said that stone walls were not legitimate hazards and that no

In 1908 a 72-hole foursome was played for £100 a side. The contestants were (left to right) Edward Ray playing with Tom Vardon (Harry's younger brother) v. George Duncan playing with C. H. Mayo, a fine, painstaking player, who later went to the States

Horace Hutchinson (1859-1932), who won the British Amateur Championship in 1886 and 1887. He learned his golf at Westward Ho! in Devon and played in the first Oxford v. Cambridge match in 1878. Subsequently he became a most respected golfing writer

shall always remember. He was a sturdy Englishman and a strong player who won the British Open five times between 1894 and 1913. The Open had been extended to 72 holes in 1893. In the twenty-two intervening years from the lengthened championship to the outbreak of World War I, the Great Triumvirate took the title between them no fewer than sixteen times.

Harry Vardon came from Jersey, in the Channel Islands. He was a prettier player to watch than Taylor – a slim figure with a perfect, rather upright swing and, like Walter Hagen later, he would bend his left arm on the back swing, which enabled him to hit the ball early, but which is also an exceptionally difficult swing to control. In the 1890s he won the British Open three times – 1896 over J. H. Taylor, 1898 over Willie Park Jr, and 1899 over Jack White. Taylor's winning years in the 1890s had been 1894, 1895 and 1900.

James Braid won his first British Open in 1901, though he had been runner-up to Harold Hilton in 1897, but I shall leave further discussion of this marvellous, tall, stooping Scot until the next chapter.

The Amateur Championship in Britain in the 1890s had been largely in the hands of three men – John Ball Jr, F. G. Tait and Harold Hilton in 1897, but I shall leave record eight times, but Harold Hilton, though victorious only three times in the Amateur, won the British Open twice as well (in 1892 and 1897) and as we shall see rocked America by taking their Amateur trophy abroad for the first time.

Before the century closes and the gutta-percha ball is replaced by Haskell's innovation, there is one mystery golfer, a professional already mentioned in passing, who with Bob Jones and Ben Hogan shares the honour of being the only man to win four US Opens.

Willie Anderson was a Scot, but his family background is not known. He was dour and uncommunicative, playing golf with a dedication similar to that of Hogan. He seemed to have had trouble finding a permanent job and his defeat by one stroke by Joe Lloyd in the 1897 US Open went almost unremarked. In the following year he finished third, in 1899 fifth, in 1900 eleventh (this was the year in which Vardon won the US Open), but in 1901 he broke through. He was at the time with the Pittsfield Country Club, Massachusetts. The Open was staged at the Myopia Hunt Club with sixty entries. Anderson tied with Alex Smith for an enormous 331, but in the play-off beat Smith by one stroke. In 1903 he won again. At Glen View Golf Club, Illinois, in 1904, he held his title, finishing in a magnificent 72 to defeat Gil Nichols by 5 strokes, and then in 1905 he capped everything by winning for the fourth time, the third time in succession, again defeating Alex Smith and again at Myopia. His run was broken in 1906 by Alex Smith, and then this strangely unsung man succumbed to a fatal lung disease and died comparatively young.

So the new century saw one of the great golfing records set up and was also to see the introduction of a new and revolutionary ball, the Haskell, which bounded along the fairways and flew off the club face without the stony shock on the hands the unresilient gutty gave to the golfer. This ball made every golfer a better player overnight, for mis-hits 'went a mile' with no pain!

3 The Great Years: 1902-19

THE COMING OF the rubber-core ball, which so changed the game of golf, was surprisingly late, considering that all the ingredients were available. Dr Coburn Haskell, an average golfer from Cleveland, Ohio, had for some time been on the look out for a substitute for gutta-percha. In 1898, touring the Goodrich Rubber factory at Akron, and noticing some narrow strips of rubber waste, he felt that here might be the answer. Fired with enthusiasm, he and Bertram Work, a friend in the company, experimented by winding stripping under tension round a solid core of rubber. At first they could not solve the problem of even winding, but a machine built by John Gammeter, an employee of the company, successfully overcame this, and having secured patents (Goodrich held shop rights) they were ready to go into business. They used a thin sheath of moulded gutta-percha for the cover, which was then painted white. The early balls suffered from an erratic 'ducking' flight which was remedied by impressing the cover with deeper markings.

There were two curious corollaries to this success story. The patents were not upheld in England, leaving production of the new wonder open to all. The great Harry Vardon spent nearly a year in 1900 advertising a super new long distance gutty from Spalding by playing exhibition matches in the States with it. The 'Vardon Flier', as it was called, may have been an improved gutty, and certainly the tour helped the cause of golf enormously in America (Vardon won the US Open at Chicago that year) but, alas, the day of the gutty was almost over, and within a short time the 'Vardon Flier' was a thing of the past, and the great golfer never saw the massive commission he had hoped for from its sale. Some in England averred that he never played golf as well again.

In 1901 Walter Travis won the American Amateur Championship with the rubber 'Bounding Billy', but it was Sandy Herd's victory, by chance using the Haskell, in the 1902 British Open by one stroke over Vardon

Not every eye on the ball, as a competitor takes a last look at the hole on the 17th green at North Berwick, Scotland. The Bass Rock is clearly visible in the background

(a record 307) that aroused the keenest interest in the new rubber-core ball.

And yet it was *not* the perfect answer. Though its greater resilience could add a good 20 yards to a shot, the same bounciness made it harder to control, and its arrival led to courses having to be lengthened. Par four with a gutty had meant a hole of 310 to 380 yards. Par four with the rubber ball meant 390–450 yards. And there was a further headache for golf-course architects. With a gutty a professional might have out-hit an 18-handicapper by 25 yards. Now the difference had increased to up to 75 yards.

There were of course many improvements to Haskell's ball (and these are detailed in some excellent histories of the golf ball) but essentially for the next seventy years the principle of golf-ball manufacture differed only in detail. Balata covers replaced gutta-percha; various cores, including liquids and steel, were tried out. One extraordinary ball, the pneumatic, appeared in 1905. This had a rubber and silk shell into which air was pumped at very high pressure and in fact this ball was used by Alex Smith to win the US Open in 1906. This ingenious sphere suffered from a disconcerting propensity to explode once the shell weakened, even in the pocket. Yet it had its very keen advocates, and it has been suggested it was too good and too cheap (25 cents) to be tolerated as a rival by the price-fixing rubber-ball manufacturers.

Alexander (Sandy) Herd, who had put the Haskell on the map, was the Great Triumvirate's closest rival. Just older than the other three, he was in contention from 1895, when he was runner-up to Taylor in the British Open, through his triumph in 1902 in the same event until 1920, when again he was runner-up, this time to George Duncan at Deal. Before the 1902 British Open at the Royal Liverpool Club's links at Hoylake in 1902, Sandy Herd played the first practice round with John Ball, who had been the first amateur to win the British Open, way back in 1890. John Ball in fact won the Amateur eight times, but the important thing for Sandy Herd

Alex ('Sandy') Herd, British Open champion in 1902, in action (1923). He was famous for his 'waggles' before hitting the ball. Three years after this photograph was taken he became British Professional Match Play champion for the second time, at the age of 58

was that his practice opponent was using the Haskell ball. Ball was doing so well with the new rubber-cored missile that Sandy Herd commented on it and, 'when we reached the 15th hole, Mr Ball, smiling at my comments regarding his drives, gave me a Haskell to try. That was the end of the gutty ball for me.' After that Herd purchased the remaining four Haskells in Jack Morris's shop (Jack was a nephew of Old Tom Morris) and then in true Hagen style proceeded to tell everyone that the new ball was useless. He won the Open, and Vardon claimed that the new ball

Right A quintet of famous British professionals. They are (from left to right) Jack White, winner of the British Open Championship in 1904, John Rowe, professional at Ashdown Forest for more than 50 years, the illustrious Harry Vardon, Albert Tingey, and Sandy Herd
Below Harry Vardon demonstrates the position of the hands for two different types of drive. On the left the hands are slightly ahead of the ball, suitable for a drive into the wind; on the right he has moved his hands back so that he can get the ball 'up' into a following wind. Notice too the positions of his left heel

had robbed him of victory, for when playing with Peter McEwen on the day of the final, and seeing the Scottish player pitching consistently short, Vardon too began to pitch his mashie shots short, and whereas McEwen's Haskell ran well, Vardon's gutty stopped dead. After that 1902 Open practically everybody switched to the Haskell.

While the British, in the main, held the field, an Australian-born American, Walter J. Travis, was startling the United States. He had only taken up the game in 1896 at the age of thirty-five, but in 1898 he had progressed as far as the semi-finals of the US Amateur. He was defeated by Findlay Douglas, and the pattern was repeated in 1899. But in 1900 he turned the tables and beat Douglas, 2 up, in the final. He was a slightly built, taciturn man, continuously smoking a long black cigar. Though he was not a long hitter, his play was deadly accurate, almost machine-like. He repeated his success in the US Amateur in 1901 and 1903, the first player to win this championship three times. In 1901 he also managed third place in the US Open. But his most extraordinary performance was at Sandwich in 1904 in the British Amateur. He had played badly in practice at St Andrews and putted badly in practice at Sandwich. He borrowed a friend's 'Schenectady' putter, a centre-shafted, mallet-headed club, and his putting improved. (The Schenectady putter was later banned for years by the Royal and Ancient.) But what was extraordinary was not the putter, or the win at Sandwich (though the achievement was a very fine one), but the treatment that was meted out to Walter Travis in England. Obviously there are two sides to the story, but on the balance of evidence it would seem that the 'Old Man', as he was called, was treated extremely shabbily by his hosts. There is no doubt that Travis's somewhat saturnine and withdrawn temperament did not endear him to the English and perhaps he could have been accused of over-brusqueness towards his would-be hosts. He had kept himself apart from offers of hospitality, but such an attitude is not un-

Left Walter Travis, first American winner of the British Amateur Championship in 1904. He also won the US Amateur title three times and was once runner-up in the US Open. He would use a centre-shafted Schenectady putter on the greens, but although this club was always legal in the United States, it was banned by the Royal and Ancient from 1909 to 1952

Above left Jerome D. Travers, US Open champion in 1915 and one of the great amateurs of all time. He won the US Amateur Championship four times and he was also an early critic of slow play. 'We have a tendency to be too deliberate,' he once wrote

Above Plenty of trouble awaits a poor drive at the 5th at England's Westward Ho!, the Royal North Devon, seen here on an October day, 1905. This course, founded in 1864, has remained on its original site longer than any other English course. J. H. Taylor was born and died here

common in sport where the sportsman is totally dedicated, as Travis was, to winning. But one must remember that not only was he not the most convivial person, but also that he was not allotted lodgings in the usual Royal St George's guest quarters, that he was not able to play practice rounds with the star British golfers, that he was presented with an almost half-witted caddie and that he was ignored by the Oxford and Cambridge players, who had been so well looked after in the United States in 1903. It is not surprising that a certain resentment seethed within him, and the course of the Championship did not improve things. In the first round he quite justifiably 'called' H. H. Holden of Hoylake on the 7th hole for grounding his iron in a sand trap. The atmosphere became icy. He completed his round at 1.50p.m., soaked to the skin in the heavy downpour. (It is strange how many of the more dramatic British matches have been played in terrible weather.) Despite a plea to change into dry clothes he was told to be on the tee for the second round at 2.28p.m. James Robb his

opponent was fresh, having had a walkover in the morning. Alas, the match was again spoilt by an incident for which Robb was in no way responsible. Travis's cross-eyed caddie picked up Travis's ball on the 11th green. Robb, sportingly, made no protest, but when after the round Travis requested another caddie, his wish was ignored. He had a 3 and 1 victory in the third round, beat a fine Irish golfer, H. E. Reade, in the fourth, having been two down with four to play, and then came up against Harold Hilton. Opinion as to Travis's skills had swung to a grudging acceptance of his remarkable accuracy, but opposed to Hilton (already the winner of two British Opens and two British Amateur Championships) it did not rate his chances very highly. In fact Hilton was not on his best form and Travis beat him quite comfortably 5 and 4. Horace Hutchinson, a great writer on golf, was the next victim, but then, the British said, Hutchinson was getting on. In the final the Old Man was to meet a man who had hit a gutty 358 yards and had 'made' the 18th green at St Andrews, Ted Blackwell.

Blackwell lost the match, 4 and 3, and Travis's clinching putt was hailed by an impenetrable silence. Of course this sort of reaction has happened since, but there is something in-human about a crowd not rising to a victor in a cleanly fought duel. Where a match has been won by default or by some obscure official ruling then there is some modicum of excuse for the gallery's lack of enthusiasm, but I think that the crowd's brutality at this stage in Travis's triumph demonstrated an enormous lapse in British manners.

The cup was presented to Travis by Lord Northbourne, who lived in a nearby castle and whose family had held land there for centuries. The peer spoke interminably about the historical glories of the county of Kent, and about British golf and golfers and hoped that such a disaster as Mr Travis's victory would never hit British sport again. It was an ungracious speech which the Old Man gracefully acknowledged.

Travis continued to play fairly good golf,

Above Mann's bunker at Royal Portrush in Northern Ireland. In 1951 it became the only course outside England and Scotland to host the Open Championship
Right James Braid putting out against Harry Vardon at Sandy Lodge, England, in 1910. Unlike Vardon and Taylor, Braid never travelled to the United States

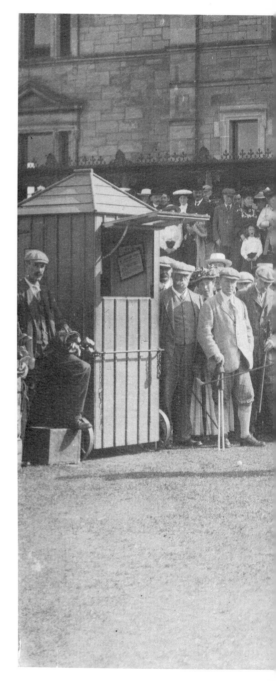

Left The redoubtable John Ball, in 1890 both the first amateur and the first Englishman to win the British Open. He also took the British Amateur title eight times. Here, in 1929, he is using one of the earliest steel-shafted clubs
Right James Braid takes one last look down the 1st fairway before driving off at St Andrews. Watching, left to right, are Alex Herd, Harry Vardon and J. H. Taylor

and especially enjoyed his matches against the young Jerome Dunstan Travers. He finally gave up tournament golf in 1915, the year in which he won the Metropolitan Open, and had meanwhile founded and edited the *American Golfer*, the renowned golfing magazine.

Jerry Travers was only seventeen years old when he beat the Old Man in the final of the Nassau Invitation tournament in 1904. From then on they beat each other and lost to each other with almost monotonous regularity. Travers's game improved immensely in these friendly needle confrontations and at twenty-one the younger man won the US Amateur, defeating Archie Graham 6 and 5 in the final. (Walter Travis was the medallist in this Amateur for the fifth time out of a total of six, which gives some measure of the deadly accuracy of the Australian.)

Travers defended his title successfully in the next year and Walter Travis, in the earliest issues of his new *American Golfer*, published the sort of commentary with pictures on the young man's game which has become so popular since in magazines and newspapers. In all, Travers won four US Amateur titles and his crowning achievement was the US Open in 1915, when he became

Left Harold Hilton, British Open champion in 1892 (the first year the Championship was played over 18 holes) and 1897, a flourishing, attacking player who would frequently lose his cap in the act of hitting the ball. He once had a handicap of plus 10 at his native Hoylake. This photograph was taken in 1910, when he won both the British Amateur (for the third out of four times) and the US Amateur Championship

Above The 18th tee at La Boulie, near Versailles, France, 1908. The great French player Arnaud Massy was for many years professional at this course

only the second amateur to take the title.

Of his play one can say that Jerry Travers was totally dedicated while on the course – unsmiling, furious at distractions and a magnificent all-round player. His putting, in his earlier years suspect, became so deadly that it could only be compared to Travis's. He also had the enviable ability to win when he was playing below form.

The early 1900s were the heyday in Britain of the Great Triumvirate. In 1900 Harry Vardon had made his first voyage to America to promote Spalding's new gutty, the 'Vardon Flier'. The American pros had a story about his visit to the States. They would tell their younger compatriots: 'He would not play the same course twice in the same day, you know.' 'Why not?' 'Because he was so accurate, that in his second round his shots finished in the divot holes he had made in the morning, and that took the fun out of the game for him.' In all his exhibition matches there he only lost once and his victory (over J. H. Taylor) in the same year in the US Open gave the fast growing American game an even greater fillip, though strangely

Above June 1912, and Abe Mitchell prepares a recovery during the British Amateur Championship at Westward Ho! In the event, he finished runner-up to John Ball
Far left Jim Barnes, one of the handful of men to have won the Open Championships of both the USA (1921) and Britain (1925), here seen driving off coconut matting in an exhibition match
Left Alex Smith, brother of Macdonald and Willie, three Carnoustie-born professionals who played a prominent part in the US Open in the early 1900s. Alex, a 'miss-'em quick' putter, was champion in 1906 and 1910

enough this great 9-stroke victory heralded a tragic slump in Vardon's game. He became subject to putting jitters (as was Ben Hogan in later years) and lost the 1900 British Open at St Andrews to Taylor by 8 strokes. He himself felt that he had left something of his finest game in America and as Bernard Darwin wrote, he 'certainly never mowed down his enemies in quite the same way again'. Nevertheless, he was runner-up in the British Open to James Braid in 1901 at Muirfield and runner-up to Sandy Herd at the Royal Liverpool, Hoylake in the following year. Then in 1903 Vardon amazingly won the British Open at Prestwick, defeating his brother Tom by 6 strokes. I say 'amazing' because Harry was so ill with a lung disease that many times he felt that he would collapse. But after a spell in a sanatorium he recovered sufficiently to continue playing, though his health suffered till his death. Despite his putting troubles and his illness, this beautiful swinger went on to win the British Open twice more (1911 and 1914), the *News of the World* Tournament (British PGA) in 1912, and was twice runner-up in the US Open in 1913 and 1920 (at the age of fifty).

There was one very special occasion when The Triumvirate and Sandy Herd came together: the great International Professional foursomes in 1905 which was played over four courses for a prize of £400 (then, $1600). Vardon and Taylor were matched against the two Scots, Braid and Herd, and after the first 36 holes at St Andrews the Scots were carried triumphantly off by their partisan supporters – they were 2 up. But at Troon, on Scotland's west coast, the Scotsmen lost the goodwill of their countrymen when Vardon and Taylor inflicted an astonishing defeat of 14 holes. At St Anne's on the Lancashire coast the Scots rallied and were only 7 down, but even Vardon's illness on the final lap at Deal could not help them. In a heavy storm the Englishmen won 13 up and 12 to play.

James Braid, 'Jimmy', as I was later allowed to call him, was the least cosmopolitan of the three. He was one of the wonders of the golfing

world. I remember when the tall, ruddy-complexioned stooping old Scot celebrated his 78th birthday in 1948 with a 74 and, as I have said elsewhere, his *super*intendence of the course at Walton Heath is something I shall always admire, even revere, and be grateful for. He was almost archetypally Scottish in his reticence – a man of few words – yet his golfing temperament was perfect. Nothing seemed to ruffle him. When he was on the PGA executive committee his few well-chosen words were always invaluable. In his later days, too, there was a charming incident when an American 'doing' the British golf courses and finding nobody to play with in the clubhouse was advised by the secretary to take out 'Jimmy'. 'Jimmy' gave him the works, and after the game, when the American was politely asked how he had liked the course, he replied that he had enjoyed it very much but was amazed at the golf 'the old fellow in the tin hut put up', adding that he must have been 'some shooter' in his youth. James Braid *was* some shooter in his youth. He was Harry Vardon's exact contemporary, a year younger than Sandy Herd and a year older than J. H. Taylor. His record was as astounding as that of his two great rivals. He became the first golfer to win five British Open Championships (between 1901 and 1910). He also won the British PGA (*News of the World* Tournament) four times, and the French Open in 1910. He only became a professional in his twenty-seventh year in 1896, and in 1897 the British Open, which he lost to Willie Park Jr, only eluded him by one stroke. As late as 1927 he was runner-up in the *News of the World* Championship.

I have mentioned the *News of the World* Tournament several times, so perhaps it would be as well to recognize its importance. The *News of the World* is a British Sunday newspaper and its sponsorship of the British PGA Match Play Championship from 1903 was an important, and professionally lucrative, addition to the golfing calendar. Until its recent change of ownership (the tournament

is now sponsored by Benson & Hedges) the newspaper continued its good work. For the record, James Braid, as we have seen, won it four times, Harry Vardon once, J. H. Taylor twice, myself three times and Peter Thomson and Dai Rees four times. However, as a match-play tournament, it somewhat conflicts with the very prestigious Piccadilly World Match Play Championship at Wentworth. Nevertheless, the British PGA Match Play should be honoured as the oldest professional tournament in the world.

J. H. Taylor was the only full-blooded Englishman of The Triumvirate. I got to know him when he was quite an old man (he lived to ninety-one), and I always admired his business-like attitude to the game. Not only did he construct dozens and dozens of golf courses with his business partner, Hawtree, but he also went into a very successful club-making business with his partner Cann.

He was much stockier than the other two, and in his heyday used a bent left arm and a very full pivot which turned his back to the hole on his backswing. Nothing about this swing was beautiful, but it was powerful and extremely effective. After his defeat by Harry Vardon in the US Open in 1900, the year in which he won the British Open for the third time, he went on to win the *News of the World* Championship twice, the French Open twice, the German Open once and two more British Opens (1909 and 1913).

Perhaps Taylor's greatest victory was at the Open at Hoylake in 1913. He had had a splendid victory over Jimmy Braid and Tom Ball (by a margin of 6 strokes) in 1909, but at Hoylake he only just qualified and then had to play in quite appalling conditions of wind and rain. Ted Ray, the hulking Jerseyman, whose play-off struggle with Francis Ouimet and Harry Vardon in the US Open

Left Arnaud Massy of France, British Open champion 1907 and four times French Open champion driving off at La Boulie, 1913
Right A historic photograph. Francis Ouimet (centre) with Harry Vardon (left) and Ted Ray, whom he defeated in a play-off for the US Open Championship at The Country Club, Brookline, in 1913. Bernard Darwin later wrote: 'It was one of the most momentous of all rounds because, in a sense, it founded the American Golfing Empire'

took place in the same year, and who was the holder of the British Open, led with 147 at the end of the first day. With Taylor one stroke behind him, they confronted the second day – a day of total devastation, with tents blown down, swirling rain, and general conditions of such magnitude that even Hoylake admitted it was a storm. Taylor, feet firmly planted and coat collar turned up, went round in 77. In the afternoon he managed 79, but he holed the 6th (the Briars) in three, in the full rage of the storm, and at the end of the day Ted Ray trailed by 8 strokes. (Even in 1924 Taylor was in contention in the British Open, finishing fifth, only 6 strokes behind Walter Hagen.)

The next year, 1914, despite later playing miraculous golf, and partly because of the war, can be considered the last year of The Triumvirate. In that year Harry Vardon left the other two behind (just) by winning his sixth Open. Jimmy Braid and J. H. Taylor had only won five!

In the States, Alex Smith, Scottish born, and friend of Willie Anderson, whose feats I have already described, was establishing various records. His 1906 victory in the US Open over his brother Willie at Oswentsia, Illinois, broke the 300 stroke barrier. In 1908 at Myopia, Massachusetts, he was defeated in the play-off for the US Open by Fred McLeod, who only weighed 7st 10lbs (108lbs), and in 1910 he won the first three-way play-off in US Open history. John J. McDermott was 4 strokes behind with a 75 and Alex's brother Mac shot a 77. Alex Smith's putting was celebrated because of its speed – so different from most of today's deliberators; as he himself would say: 'Miss'em quick.'

Far from the English-speaking pioneers, in Biarritz, was a remarkable Frenchman with Basque blood, Arnaud Massy. Massy's win

Left A tough lie for Ted Ray in the 1923 British Open at Troon— though not tough enough to make him remove his pipe! This Open was the last to be won by a Briton (Arthur Havers) until Henry Cotton's 1934 win

Above Better not to stray from the fairways at Walton Heath, England, as James Braid discovers. Braid was professional there for 45 years. This photograph was taken in 1922

at Hoylake, to take the British Open in 1907, so delighted him that he christened his daughter (born the following year) Hoylake Massy. He was a huge man with a volatile temperament, but his prowess was not in doubt. He was runner-up (beaten in the play-off by Harry Vardon) in the British Open in 1911 and in fact had been coached at North Berwick by Ben Sayers, the tiny acrobat, whose ability to play in wind was renowned.

By 1913 America was poised for the real breakthrough in the popularity of golf. The Country Club, Brookline, Massachusetts, was smart and it was the home of one of the earliest American golf clubs (1892). In 1913 it was to become the scene of perhaps the most dramatic US Open ever played. Harry Vardon was there, on his second tour of the United States, and with him from England was the powerful, bulky Ted Ray, who had won the British Open at Muirfield the year before and was still in fact the holder and who had clearly outplayed Vardon, Braid and Taylor on that occasion. The US Open at Brookline had been postponed to allow these two to compete after their exhibition tour. There was a record 165 entries. The Atlantic

59

Above An intent gallery watch James Braid putt on the 15th green during the 1923 British Open at Troon

Left Pipe as always clamped between his teeth, Ted Ray plays to the 4th green during the 1923 British Open at Troon

but for a 5 on the 16th at Sandwich (he steered his ball into a trap), he might have claimed his third victory. In fact he finished only a stroke behind Vardon and Massy, who tied for first place. America was perturbed by 'Childe Harold's Pilgrimage', as it was dubbed. Since H. M. Harriman in 1899, the Amateur had been won by homebred Americans. Now it was endangered. There had been rivalry between western and eastern states at the championship, but united by a common enemy even Chicago, where the match was being played, did not object to an easterner stifling the threat from abroad. Hilton reached the final to play against an amiable giant, Fred Herreshoff. Hilton won in a sudden death play-off on the 37th, but his manner of winning became famous. Herreshoff had clouted a long drive and Hilton's slightly faded shot gave him the next

stroke. He took a spoon, gave his characteristic little toe spring, and lashed the wood down. A bad shot, and the ball careered away towards a rocky bank. It crashed into the bank and rolled gently down – on to the green. He would get his 4, whereas Herreshoff, no doubt unnerved by this display, had a 20-foot putt to make for a possible half. He did not make it. It was an odd ending and people tried to detract from the triumph of Hilton's victory. But like it or not, the cup left the States for the first time. It was some consolation that in 1911 the first native American, Johnny McDermott, won the Open.

McDermott had been runner-up in the American Open in 1910 and retained the title at Buffalo in 1912, so as defending champion in 1913 he had been as outraged as everyone else in the locker room at The Country Club before Ouimet's famous victory, when a cocky twenty-year-old Hagen, whom he did not know from Adam, strode over to him and said that he'd 'come down to help you fellows stop Vardon and Ray'. McDermott was a shy, small, big-chested man (only 130lbs – 9st 4lbs) who expected to win every tournament, but although he beat Vardon in the 1913 Shawnee Open, his nerves suddenly snapped and he had to retire from professional golf in 1915.

Chick Evans was undoubtedly the greatest amateur golfer of his generation. He was born in 1890 and later played in many Walker Cup matches and became a frequent and popular visitor to Britain. But by 1912 he had never really got the luck he felt he deserved, dropping out in the semi-finals in 1909, 1910 and 1911. In 1912 he was soundly beaten 7 and 6 by Jerry Travers. In 1913, after a sensationally good year in the northwest, he was out again in the semi-finals. In 1914 he had his second stab, with no luck, at the British Amateur. It was his putting that consistently let him down. In 1914 he lost the US Open by one stroke to Walter Hagen who won his first major championship. In the same year he did not even reach the semi-finals of the Amateur – taking 20 putts in the first nine holes against his opponent's (Eben Byers's) 10. In 1915 in the US Amateur he did not even survive the first round.

Then came 1916. The twenty-six-year-old ex-caddie from Chicago, with a volatile temperament, whom all the crowd liked, played 286 strokes in the Open at Minikahda and won with a record score which was to stand for twenty years, putting Jock Hutchison into second place by 2 strokes and Jim Barnes into third by 4. And now he was ready to go. He had won the Western Amateur four times (1909, 1912, 1914, 1915) and was to win it a further four times (1920–3), and he had won the Western Open in 1910, but at last he had a major title. Then at the Merion Cricket Club he took the US Amateur, beating Bob Gardner 4 and 3. He was only the third amateur to win the Open and the first golfer in history to capture both

events in one year. So he was the best, and even a bitter squabble between his fans and Ouimet's about their relative merits did little to dampen his enthusiasm.

With the war he devoted his weekends to exhibitions for charities and in 1918 raised $300,000. When his regular amateur partner, Warren Wood, became ill, he was joined by the fifteen-year-old Bob Jones.

The war over, Chick Evans again took the Amateur in 1920 at Roslyn, NY, now putting brilliantly, and convincingly beating Francis Ouimet 7 and 6, with the fast-rising star Bob Jones taking the medal with 154. Evans continued to play first-class golf for many years, losing to Jess W. Sweetser in the Amateur in 1922, medallist in 1923 with 149 (tying with Bob Jones) and beaten by Bob Jones 8 and 7 in the final in 1927. He was in the successful Walker Cup team (the first ever) in 1922, playing both foursome and singles, in 1924 in the singles, and played in the singles and partnered Bob Jones in 1928, when the USA defeated Britain by 11 to 1.

The two war years had, for America, not been as traumatic as for Europe, but nevertheless the USGA felt it right to cancel the national championships, and most of the first-class golf played was exhibition matches to raise money for charities. The USPGA, formed in 1916, followed suit and performances by the professionals were given free.

There was an unpleasant episode when Francis Ouimet was deprived of his amateur status by the none too energetic USGA for running a sports shop. This highly criticized decision was accepted by Francis Ouimet with impeccable good manners, but by summer 1917 he had had enough and played in the Western Amateur. His was a highly popular victory and the progressive Western Golf Association's sense in letting him play was admirable. Walter Travis, who had lost his amateur status through writing a column in the *American Golfer* (the magazine he founded), violently attacked the USGA and its president, Woodward, calling it high-

The tiny British music-hall star, Little Tich during a Stage Golf Tournament at Wimbledon. He died in 1928 at the age of 59

handed, intensely conservative and archaic. Francis Ouimet was reinstated.

Britain, more exhausted than America after the war, realized how powerful a challenge her golfers would have to face from across the Atlantic. She had among her leading professionals Abe Mitchell, George Duncan, two Whitcombes, Charles and Ernest, Ted Ray and the veteran Sandy Herd – the man who had shot 19 holes-in-one. And the amateurs looked good with Roger Wethered, Cyril Tolley and Tommy Armour. America, marshalling her troops for the invasion had, of course, Walter Hagen, Mike Brady, Jim Barnes and Jock Hutchison, with Leo Diegel as a young hopeful, and among her amateurs they had a great fistful with Chick Evans, Francis Ouimet, Bob Jones, Bob Gardner, Max Marston and Jesse Guilford.

4 The Transatlantic Years: 1920-45

AS THE PAINFUL MEMORIES of war slowly receded, the game of golf was to find itself dominated by America. In a final flicker of British glory, Ted Ray, at the age of forty-three, won the US Open in 1920 at Toledo by one stroke from Harry Vardon (a slowly fading fifty-year-old) who tied with Jack Burke, Jock Hutchison and Leo Diegel. There had been a record 265 contestants. Ray was the oldest competitor to win the US Open and the second and last Briton until Tony Jacklin's victory in 1969. Vardon had been leading by 5 strokes when, on the tee of the long 12th, a gale suddenly whipped up from nowhere. His strength was no longer great enough and in those last seven holes he dropped seven strokes. He never won a major title again. As a memorial to one of the greatest of golfers the annual Harry Vardon Trophy is awarded to the American and British professionals with the best playing average.

The growth of the popularity of golf meant more standardization of rules and centralization of its management. The Royal and Ancient took over the organization of the British Amateur and Open in 1920, and in 1921 the Rules Committee of the Royal and Ancient and the USGA jointly brought in the important Limitation of the Ball amendment to the rules. The ball was now to weigh no more than 1.62oz and to be no less than 1.62in. in diameter. So again a change in the ball neatly coincided with the start of a new era.

There were two outstanding British golfers in 1921, Abe Mitchell and George Duncan. Both were in their thirties, Mitchell simply hitting the ball beautifully, time after time, Duncan inspired but erratic. (It was Abe Mitchell who coined the phrase 'a golfer must always move freely beneath himself'.) They had tied on the Old Course at St Andrews in the earliest important post-war British tournament. In 1920 at Deal, in the first post-war British Open, Duncan beat off Sandy Herd by two strokes. Next year, however, the American-domiciled Scottish professional, Jock Hutchison, took the cup to America for

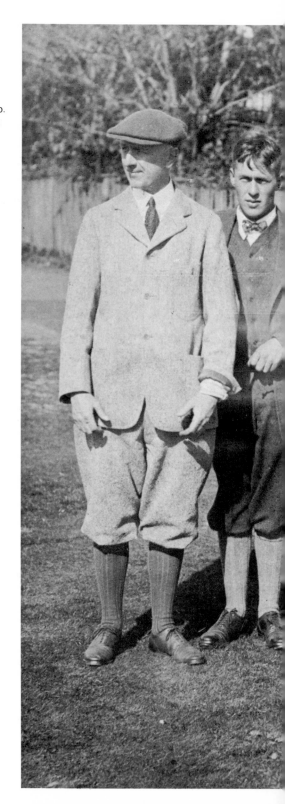

Bob Jones, second from left, on his first appearance in Britain, in 1921. He was a member of an American amateur team that played, and beat, Britain 9 to 3 at Hoylake. A year later the match became known as the Walker Cup. With him, left to right, are William Fownes (the captain), Wood Platts, Fred Wright, Francis Ouimet, Paul Hunter and Jesse Guilford

the first time, beating the elegant amateur Roger Wethered by 9 strokes in the play-off. It was the first time the cup had left Britain since the Frenchman, Arnaud Massy's, win in 1907 at Hoylake.

But though Britain managed to retain her Amateur Championship, despite a large contingent of Americans taking part (including Bob Jones who was beaten 6 and 5 in the fourth round by an elderly gentleman called Allan Graham), neither Duncan nor Mitchell had managed to make any impression on the US Open at the Columbia Country Club,

where Long Jim Barnes had set a fast pace to beat Walter Hagen and Fred McLeod by 9 strokes. Barnes, an immensely tall and lanky Cornish-bred American, had further success as runner-up in the British Open in 1922 (this time beaten by Hagen) and as winner of the British Open in 1925.

America's total triumph was achieved in 1922. Twice winner of the US Open, Walter Hagen, the 'character' with a greater following than perhaps any golfer except Arnold Palmer in the 1960s, won the British Open at Sandwich. Though Jock Hutchison had

Above Walter Hagen putts against Abe Mitchell at Gleneagles, Scotland, in 1921, in an international match between Britain and America. It was a forerunner of the Ryder Cup, instituted 6 years later

Right Abe Mitchell, who has often been referred to as the greatest golfer never to have won the British Open. Three times British Professional Match Play champion, he became with George Duncan and Ted Ray the immediate successors to the original triumvirate of Vardon, Braid and Taylor. Here he is seen playing at Deal, England, 1920

taken the cup to the States, he was after all a native of St Andrews. Hagen was American through and through and Sandwich was a new achievement in his great reign. He led with 149 after two rounds. With a poor round of 78 he was tied with Charles Whitcombe and Jim Barnes, only one stroke behind Jock Hutchison. Typically he pulled out all stops and produced a 'Hagen finish' of 72. It looked like victory, one stroke ahead of Barnes, but he still had to reckon with the erratic George Duncan, now producing a run of inspired play. On the 72nd tee Duncan had played 64 strokes. A 4 on the last hole would have given him a tie with Hagen, but a snatched chip robbed him, and he had to be content to share second place with Jim Barnes.

So with the British Open firmly in Uncle Sam's pocket, the new spirit in American golf awaited its new heroes – and they soon came. The US Open of 1922 at Skokie, Illinois, was won by a twenty-year-old caddie, of Italian parents, Gene Sarazen. Sarazen, whose father was an immigrant carpenter-contractor named Saraceni, was a short (5ft 5in.), congenial young man, with great natural intelligence. His career and popularity have lasted into the 1970s and few addicts will forget his hole-in-one in the British Open at Troon on the west coast of Scotland in 1973.

There was another fabulous feat of Gene's, but I shall come to that later. At Skokie he was an outsider; yet in that year he not only defeated a record number of contestants (including Bob Jones who tied with John Black for runner-up), but he finished with a record-tying 68 (the other 68s were Walter Hagen's in 1914 and Jock Hutchison's in 1916), also defeated the Haig 3 and 2 in a 72-hole challenge match *and* defeated Emmett French 4 and 3 in the PGA Championship at Oakmont. Quite a year for an 'unknown' who was to become a link between Vardon and the modern game. Perhaps not quite as unknown as all that, for he had beaten Jock Hutchison early in the 1921 PGA tournament and in the same year had won the New Orleans Open, but only Gene, they say, was sure he would win the US Open. Fame at last – and then he sank into ten years of failure. Perhaps he was overconfident, perhaps he worried too much about *how* he played – the pattern is not uncommon and Bob Jones had suffered from something similiar between 1917 and 1923, though in the latter year he clinched the Open which had eluded him.

Robert Tyre (Bob) Jones was possibly the greatest player golf has seen. An amateur, with an impeccable style and (acquired) tem-

Above left Arthur Havers on his way to winning the British Open at Troon, Scotland, in 1923. In the same year, touring America, he

defeated both Bob Jones and
Gene Sarazen
Above J. F. Neville, of the United
States, attempts to play out of a
burn in the Walker Cup foursomes
at St Andrews in 1923. The
American team won 6 to 5

perament, in the seven years of his glory (1923–30) he won four US Opens, five US Amateurs, three British Opens and one British Amateur. From 1922 to 1930, when he retired, he played in nine US Opens and three British Opens. Only in 1927 did he not win or come second in the US Open and in 1930 he achieved the Grand Slam – the US Open and Amateur and the British Open and Amateur – a feat never accomplished before or since. (During his tournament days his constant mentor and chronicler was O. B. Keeler, with whom he travelled altogether 120,000 miles, and it was Keeler who 'invented' the 'seven lean years and seven fat years' of Jones's golfing career the fat years starting in 1923.) He had won his first tournament (6 holes) when he was six, beating, among others, Alexa Stirling (who was to win the US Women's Amateur Championship in 1916, 1919 and 1920 and was runner-up in 1921, runner-up and medallist in 1923 and medallist in 1925). And his

success just grew. By the age of fourteen, in 1916, he had won the Georgia state tournament, though his temper was erratic. At seventeen he was beaten in the finals of the US Amateur by Davison Herron 5 and 4; at eighteen, in 1920, though winning the qualifying medal at Roslyn, New York, he was beaten in the semi-finals by Francis Ouimet (defeated in the final by Chick Evans). Then in 1922, the year before his first major success, he went to England as the youngest member of the Walker Cup team.

The birth of the Walker Cup came after World War I. It was born from matches played between the United States and Canada. In 1914 The Royal Canadian Golf Association had invited the USGA to an amateur tournament. It is perhaps not surprising that the American ten defeated Canada 12 to 3 at Hamilton, Ontario. The team consisted of John G. Anderson, Eben Byers, Chick Evans, Robert Gardner, Bob Jones, Oswald

Above Gene Sarazen, who two
years earlier had won the US
Open Championship, begins his
challenge for the 1924 British
Open at Hoylake. He had to wait
until 1932 to achieve his ambition

Kirkby, Max Marston, Francis Ouimet, George Ormiston and Jerome Travers, with Bill Fownes as captain. There was a return match in the following year, again with an American victory. In 1920 the USGA crossed to Britain to discuss the modification of rules, and on their return the idea of international matches was put forward. George Walker of the National Golf Links of America was so taken with the scheme that he offered an International Challenge Trophy which was soon known simply as the Walker Cup. But though the USGA hopefully invited all possible countries to send teams to the States in 1921, none could accept and only an informal contest took place that year at Hoylake, England, between America and Britain. America's success was almost total – they beat the British in all the four foursomes and won five of the eight singles. Next year, the Royal and Ancient decided to send a team to the United States, where curiously Bernard Darwin, the greatest of all writers on golf, travelling as correspondent for *The Times* of London, found himself playing when the British captain withdrew through illness and beating Bill Fownes, the American

captain, 3 and 1. But the home team took the cup. From then on the Walker Cup became a regular event, held, after 1924, biennially, in the even years, alternating with the professional Ryder Cup, which was first officially played in 1927. Since World War II the Walker Cup has been played in the uneven years – coinciding with the Ryder Cup.

For Britain there was one gleam of light in 1923. Arthur Havers, the twenty-five-year-old Coombe Hill professional, who before the war had qualified for the British Open at the age of sixteen, found himself ahead in the British Open at Troon after three rounds of 73. Joe Kirkwood, an Australian who later went to America and astonished people by his trick shots, trailed by one, while Walter Hagen trailed by two, one ahead of Macdonald Smith. Arthur Havers managed a competent 76 in the fourth round and only Hagen was near enough to take him, but a sliced second shot on the 18th was bunkered, and the Championship went to a Briton for the last time until I regained it in 1934.

Meanwhile Walter Hagen, though not particularly successful in 1923 (runner-up in both the British Open and the PGA), was consolidating his position as the greatest professional in the world. He was not a perfect golfer but I always admired his attitude towards the golfing world and his financial success. More than anyone else, though I had a part in the process myself, he released the professional from the attitude which had relegated him to a position 'below the salt' in the golfing hierarchy. His bland indifference to what people expected of a professional's subservience to the members (amateur) of golf clubs, his ability, to a larger extent than mine, to combine in his greatest years an extremely social life with phenomenal playing when he most needed it, and his whole lifestyle, which presupposed that 'Sir' Walter was the object of adulation even in the presence of his friend the Prince of Wales, seemed to bring a fresh current of air through the stuffier corridors of the game. Only in the

Wyant Vanderpeel (left) presents the Walker Cup in 1924 to Robert Gardner, captain of the successful American team, while Cyril Tolley, the British captain, looks on

Ernest Whitcombe, eldest of three well-known British golfing brothers, playing in the 1923 British Open at Hoylake. He was runner-up to Walter Hagen. Ernest, and his brothers Charles and Reggie, were all members of the 1935 Ryder Cup team

'Wild Bill' Mehlhorn, who played for the United States in the first Ryder Cup match, 1927, here contests the British Open in the same year at St Andrews, driving from the 4th tee

attitude of many clubs to women has that 1920s–1930s intolerant stance persisted (though it is not so long ago that certain 'smart' clubs would refuse Jewish members and, outside Scotland, prolonged the differences between 'artisan' players and 'members'). Walter never trained hard until his later years, when his ability to putt deserted him and he had to polish it up, but he was one of the greatest of all gamesmen on the course and the stories are legion. Always ready to have a party, the tale is told by Bernard Darwin of a late-night card session at the Marine Hotel, Gullane, during the 1929 British Open at Muirfield. By 3 or 4a.m., one of his supporters, hoping to persuade 'the Haig' to get some sleep, said that Leo Diegel, at that moment his nearest rival, had been abed for some hours. 'But', replied Hagen, 'he won't be asleep.' And, given Diegel's nervous nature, how true that probably was!

I did not actually meet Hagen until 1928, though I had seen him play in 1926, the year that he beat Bob Jones at Sarasota and Pasadena in a 72-hole match by 12 and 11 – a year, incidentally, when he also won the National PGA Championship (for the third year running), the Western Open, the Eastern Open, and defeated Abe Mitchell in an unofficial World's Championship.

I feel that Hagen deserved his success, though he never really loved the game. Part of his success undoubtedly lay in what A. C. M. Croome called his realization that '3 of these and 1 of those still make 4'. He was not beyond reproach, but he never consciously hurt anybody. He made lifelong friends and his later years, overweight, bespectacled, do not rub off for me the glamour of my first golf hero. But in a sense Henry Longhurst was right when he wrote in 1952: 'Yet for all that, it is Hagen, the man, who will be remembered more than Hagen, the golfer.' And went on to say: '. . . Hagen's golf was very much in keeping with Hagen, the man. It had about it a fallibility combined with impertinence that endeared him to the "common man" of golf and caused him to be followed by huge galleries irrespective of his chance of success. People crowded to be with Hagen while he took 80, while the winner holed the course almost unaccompanied in 67.'

Right In 1926 Bob Jones played one of the most historic strokes in golf. Bunkered 176 yards from the 17th hole (the 71st of the Championship) at Royal Lytham, he managed to hit the green and get a 4 to creep ahead of the astounded Al Watrous, who 3-putted. This was the first of Jones's three British Opens, and this plaque, whose erection was suggested by Henry Cotton, marks the spot of the shot that won it

Below right The Ryder Cup, contested every two years by professional teams representing the United States and the United Kingdom. It is made of solid gold and was presented by Sam Ryder, a British seed merchant. The first match was held at Worcester, Massachusetts, in 1927

Overleaf Bob Jones successfully defends the British Open in 1927. Here he is putting on the 18th green at St Andrews. Jones led from the start, and on the last round took only 24 shots from the 6th tee to the 12th hole

Before closing the Hagen story one should remember his record: eleven major titles and thirteen semi-major titles. And as a final example of his gamesmanship, in 1919 in the US Open at Brae Burn, Hagen needed a birdie 3 on the last hole to win over Mike Brady who was home with 301. With a magnificent midiron shot to the green, the Haig called out his opposition to watch his 8-foot putt. Brady, shaking with nerves, watched. Hagen missed by a half-inch. On the next day, in the 18-hole play-off, Hagen infuriated Mike Brady by commenting: 'Mike, I notice you've got your sleeves rolled up. You should roll them down so the gallery won't see your muscles quivering.' The greatest pro won the play-off by one stroke.

Bob Jones (he never liked the name Bobby and preferred Bob, though even some American writers use the longer nickname) was the supreme putter. He seldom won by great margins and sometimes went down badly, but his wry-necked putter often did the trick. For shots through the green he used an extraordinarily narrow stance, which thousands tried to copy, usually disastrously, and employed a long, lazy swing, hitting the ball with a hooking flight, creating ever narrower stances as his shots became shorter. He was world famous before he was twenty – only approached as a boy wonder by Horton Smith, perhaps, who in 1928–30 was in a class of his own, eventually overshadowed by Bob Jones's 1930 Grand Slam. Some idea of Jones's usual consistency can be gauged from a memorable phrase by Kerr Petrie, writing in the New York *Herald Tribune*, after Bob's 66 in the third round of the Southern Open at East Lake in 1927: 'They wound up the Mechanical Man of Golf yesterday and sent him clicking round the East Lake course.'

I have jumped forward a little. 'Long' Jim Barnes won the British Open in 1925, giving the Cornish-born American every major pro championship in the world. Archie Compston, who once beat Hagen 18 and 17 over 72 holes, and Ted Ray were runners-up. And in 1926, as I have said, Walter Hagen beat Bob Jones

at Wentworth, but Jones took, for the first time ever, both the US Open and the British Open in that year, beating Joe Turnesa at Scioto, Columbus, Ohio by one stroke and Al Watrous at Lytham St Anne's in Lancashire. In the qualifying round for the British Open, at Sunningdale, Bob Jones shot what has been considered the most perfect round ever played in the British Isles, and certainly what he himself considered his finest competitive round. The score card ran as follows:

```
OUT Par   554 344 434 – 36
Jones     444 334 434 – 33
IN Par    544 353 444 – 36 – 72
Jones     434 343 444 – 33 – 66
```

Britain and America staged a professionals' match in the same year at Wentworth, where Britain won by 13 to 1, but it was in 1927 that the first official Ryder Cup Match was played. Samuel A. Ryder, a British seed merchant, donated a gold trophy for the event and one of his stipulations was that not only should each member of the competing teams be a member of his country's PGA but that he must be a native-born citizen of that country. In a pre-Ryder Cup team match at Wentworth there was only one victory for the USA when 'Wild' Bill Mehlhorn won a singles. Even Hagen was soundly beaten by George Duncan. And this was a warning to Hagen, for in the second Ryder Cup proper, in 1929, the story goes that the Haig arranged the pairings with George Duncan, heading the British, so that they would meet one another. Boasting, the Haig told his American team mates, 'Well, boys, that's a sure point for us.' George Duncan crushed Hagen 10 and 7; Gene Sarazen was decisively put down by Archie Compston 6 and 4. Leo Diegel and Horton Smith were the only US winners, with Al Espinosa halving his match. It was a 7 to 5 victory for the British team at Moortown. I won my singles match against Al Watrous 4 and 3.

Improvements to equipment still continued. Hickory-shafted clubs had been the only

permitted clubs until the 1920s. In 1924 the USGA allowed the use of steel-shafted putters for the first time and two years later steel shafts generally were allowed in the United States. But it was not until 1929 that the Royal and Ancient tolerated such an innovation, and when Horton Smith, then twenty years old, first came to Britain to compete in the Ryder Cup in 1929 he had to switch from his accustomed steel to the torsioned hickory – a disconcerting experience for him. As we have seen he won, over Fred Robson, though in the same year I beat him over 36 holes by 4 and 3 at Coulsdon Court GC, where Leslie, my brother, was professional and again on the same course by an identical margin the following year. He later had an accident to his wrist and never really recovered his form, but he was, with his short swing and a curious left-knee action, one of the all-time great golfers, not nowadays appreciated as he should have been. He had three glorious years in 1928–30, finishing, in 1929, worse than fourth in only four out of nineteen tournaments. The 'Joplin Ghost', as a sportswriter named him, was the leading money earner in 1929 and went on to win the

Above A kiss for the winner as Walter Hagen's wife embraces him after his victory in the 1924 British Open at Hoylake. Hagen nearly missed playing at all, for his first qualifying round was a dangerously high 83
Top right A golfer must frequently improvise. Here Walter Hagen plays left-handed from the wall beside the 9th fairway at Muirfield in 1929. The grip is orthodox, and he went on to win this British Open for a second successive year.
Bottom right Hagen uses a fairway wood as he qualifies for the 1923 British Open at Troon

first Masters at Augusta in 1934, defeating Craig Wood by one stroke. (Bob Jones and Walter Hagen tied in that maiden event, 10 strokes behind Smith.) In 1936 he took the Masters again, defeating Harry Cooper in foul weather conditions. In the same year he topped the money winners with $7,884.75. He was a veteran of twenty-seven! His colleagues thought a lot of his judgement and he later became USPGA President 1952–4.

Though Bob Jones was supreme among amateur, indeed all golfers, there was not the general difference in standard between amateurs and professionals that is apparent today – not surprisingly in view of the amount of practice and tournament play that the pros can get. I have already mentioned Roger Wethered. His trouble was his driving, otherwise he might well be considered among the all-time greats. Henry Longhurst has said that Wethered's driving was about on a par with Harry Vardon's putting: 'Just as Vardon missed occasionally and "unaccountably" from one yard, so did Wethered from time to time unloose a tee shot which earned the awe of the spectators for its splendid inaccuracy.' But he won the British Amateur at Deal in 1923 and was runner-up in 1928 and 1930, when Bob Jones, hot on the heels of his Grand Slam, defeated him 7 and 6. Roger's great rival and friend was Cyril Tolley. Tolley, three years older than Wethered, won the British Amateur in 1920 and 1929. In *1950* he was defeated by Frank Stranahan in the semi-finals. He also won two French Opens over 72 holes, though he was at his best in 18-hole matches. This 'majestic' pipe-smoking player, who so successfully struggled to subdue an unruly temperament, possessed a supple, classical swing – open to shut – using a baseball or double-handed grip, which he put to good use in his beautiful performance against Bob Gardner at the 1920 British Amateur at Muirfield. Bob Gardner, his opponent in the finals, was a fine all-round athlete who held the world pole vault record, had won the US National Amateur in 1909 at the age of

Left Len Nettlefold, a left-hander who won the Tasmanian Amateur Championship seven times and the Australian twice. Good left-handers are rare in golf, the best known being Bob Charles. Harry Vardon was proficient on his 'wrong' side, and as photographs in this book testify both Hagen and Gary Player got out of awkward spots by playing left-handed

Right The US Ryder Cup team of 1931. Back row: left to right, Horton Smith, Craig Wood, Densmore Shute, Johnny Farrell and 'Wiffy' Cox; front row: Leo Diegel, Gene Sarazen, Walter Hagen, Al Espinosa and Billie Burke. The US team won 9 to 3

Left Roger Wethered hacks his way clear of a bunker during the British Amateur Championship at Hoylake in 1927. An erratic driver but a superb iron player, he only once won the British Amateur Championship (1923), though he was twice runner-up. He was elected Captain of the Royal and Ancient in 1946

Above Not much room here as spectators crowd the burn by the 1st green at St Andrews. They are watching Bob Jones play Roger Wethered in the final of the British Amateur Championship, *en route* to his Grand Slam, 1930. Jones defeated Wethered in the final 7 and 6, over 36 holes

nineteen and was runner-up to Chick Evans in 1916. Tolley, 3 up and 4 to play, overshot the green and Gardner took this hole and the next. The 35th hole was halved as Gardner's superbly faded cleek to the pin at the last hole necessitated a sudden death play-off. The 1st hole was a short one then and Gardner, whose honour it was, dropped his tee shot on to the green. Tolley dropped his inside. Gardner's putt was laid dead and Tolley hit his straight into the back of the cup. There's a story that Tolley handed his caddie a victory five-pound note *before* he putted – a somewhat 'Haig' gesture. To the end of his playing days Tolley was capable of beating any amateur of his own age.

Ernest (later Sir Ernest) Holderness was another fine British Amateur, but his work for the Civil Service hardly allowed him time to practise. He managed to find the time, however, to take the British Amateur twice, 1922 and 1924.

There was another 'fair amateur' (Gene Sarazen's phrase) at this time, a Scot, Tommy Armour. Tommy, with whom I played a lot of golf, had lost an eye in World War I. He was then an atrocious putter, 'the three putt king', but his long game was immaculate. After playing in the first International Amateur match against the States in 1921 he went to the States in 1922 with the unofficial Walker Cup team. He stayed there and in 1924 turned professional, and though his amateur play had put him into the international class, his professional play astonished everyone. He first really showed his form in the US Open in 1927. This was the Open when Bob Jones came nowhere, but the competition was stiff enough without him, and Tommy Armour found himself up against Emmett French, Gene Sarazen, 'Wild' Bill Mehlhorn and Harry Cooper. The Open was at Oakmont and on the famous 12th (the 66th hole) the 'Silver Scot' played an abominable 7 strokes. Now he had to finish two under par to tie with Cooper and on the final hole he dropped a splendid 10-foot putt to do it and subsequently won the play-off. In the same year he won the Canadian Open. For the record, his earliest win was in the French Open Amateur Championship in 1920. He played for the States in the first International Professional Match between the USA and Britain in 1926, and after his two opens in 1927 went on to win the National PGA in 1930, the Canadian Open again, the British Open at Carnoustie in 1931 and the Canadian Open for the third time in 1934. At Carnoustie I was also playing, and after two rounds was in joint lead with the very fine Argentinian, José Jurado. Johnny Farrell, Gene Sarazen, Mac Smith and Tommy were close behind us. The Duke of Windsor was there and most eyes seemed to be fixed on José, with whom the Duke loved to air his Spanish. On the last day I had dropped out with a 79, but Jurado was still in the lead and Mac Smith was three behind with 223. Tommy, Gene and Percy Alliss had taken 225. The Silver Scot then played a magnificent round of 71, leaving

Left José Jurado, of Argentina, takes a rest as he waits for an official to give a ruling during the 1928 British Open at Sandwich. His ball lay under a bench. Jurado was seven times Open champion of Argentina and runner-up to Tommy Armour in the 1931 British Open Championship
Above Walter Hagen holes his last putt to take the 1928 British Open at Royal St George's, Sandwich

A woman spectator attempts to jump the Swilcan Burn at St Andrews in the rush to see Bob Jones's defeat of Roger Wethered in the final of the British Amateur, 1930

Jurado a 75 to win. But the Argentinian made a sad mistake. Not playing well, he had left himself 4 for a tie on the last hole. Had someone told him this, had he found out, or perhaps had his command of English been better, he would not have made such a tragic error. Instead of trying for the green with his second shot, he played short with an iron, and holed out for a 5. Tommy had won. Jurado had been a popular visitor to Britain, with his courteous manners. One of his odder characteristics was the taking of a divot as big as a straw hat with nearly every iron shot, and Tom Webster caught him beautifully in some of his cartoons. Mac Smith, incidentally, made Carnoustie a double tragedy, for, with 3–4–5 to tie with Armour, he sadly limped in with 6–5–5 in front of his own home-town supporters.

We saw in 1928 the largest entry ever assembled for the US National Open – 1064. It was the year for the immaculate Johnny Farrell. He tied Bob Jones, who was somewhat preoccupied with a new law practice,

and won the 36-hole play-off (the first time the play-off was over 36 holes). In the following year, during the Ryder Cup match played at Moortown near Leeds in England, Farrell lost to Charles Whitcombe in the singles, 8 and 6. But in the foursomes, playing against Charles again and Archie Compston, and partnered by Joe Turnesa, on a horribly cold day, when Turnesa, according to Bernard Darwin 'had the air of a poor little shivering Italian greyhound', Johnny produced an extraordinary shot which few who saw it would forget. Turnesa badly hooked his second shot on the 18th, and when at last the ball was traced Farrell was confronted with the refreshment marquee looming between him and the green. After an agitated perambulation to see how he lay, he played straight over the marquee. The shot struck the flagstick and rolled a few yards from the hole. Joe Turnesa knocked it in. The match was halved, but in fact the States lost 5 to 7. Later in the year, at Muirfield, Hagen won the British Open with Johnny Farrell as runner-

Bob Jones comes home. He walks from Battery to City Hall where he was to receive the key to New York City, recognition of his victories in the British Open and Amateur Championships of 1930

up. This, the fourth of the Haig's British Open Championship titles was in fact his last major victory. He was thirty-seven years old.

The year 1929 was, as it were, the one that Bob Jones did not do anything in the US Amateur. Instead he was put out in the first round by Johnny Goodman. Goodman had had a miserably poor early life, son of a Polish American family from Omaha. He had been a caddie for four years, but his determination to attend night schools to enable him to graduate from high school left him little time for golf. All the same he had shown himself to be the finest player in Omaha and in 1929, at the age of nineteen, he went to try his hand in the Amateur at Pebble Beach, California. And here he defeated the great Jones. He had to wait until 1937 before winning the US Amateur, but he was runner-up to the Canadian C. Ross Somerville in 1932, and in 1933 became the fifth amateur in history to win the US Open, defeating Ralph Guldahl by one stroke and becoming the third amateur to break par in the Open.

'Sandy' Somerville was a fine all-round athlete, a beautiful player to watch, with a free swing and superb iron shots. He won the 1932 US Amateur on his fifth try and became the first player since Harold Hilton in 1911 to take the Amateur Championship Trophy out of the States, but it was Goodman's US Open that really shook the pundits. Not since the Englishman Cyril Walker, professional at Englewood, beat Bob Jones in the US Open at Oakland in 1924 had such shudders rippled round the professional ranks.

Again, and inevitably, I have jumped out of a strict chronological sequence. There's Bob Jones's Grand Slam, the introduction of the 'balloon' ball and Gene Sarazen's double eagle.

Bob Jones was delighted in 1930 to be off to Britain as captain of the Walker Cup team, since it gave him a chance to play in the two British championships, and he was particularly keen to win the British Amateur — something that he had not yet added to his titles. In the Walker Cup at Royal St George's,

Sandwich, the American team won 10 to 2 with Bob playing some marvellous stuff and winning both the foursomes and the singles (against Roger Wethered 9 and 8).

Off to the Amateur at St Andrews; he had a dangerous first round against an ex-coal miner from Nottingham, Syd Roper. Though playing well (5 under par after 5 holes), he only won by 3 and 2. In the fourth round against Cyril Tolley, the match everyone wanted to see, he played in a near gale, with the sand whipping off the ridges of the bunkers. Apart from a topped drive off the first tee, Tolley played miraculously and neither player could get more than a hole's advantage in this to-and-fro fight. With the wind behind them both players overdrove the 314-yard 12th. After 16 holes they were level. Then at the 17th, the Road Hole, Jones's drive bounded across the green, towards the infamous road or the 18th tee, when it struck a greenside spectator and bounced back to land on the apron of the green. A chip and an 8-foot putt halved what had seemed to be a lost hole. The 18th was halved. Then the extraordinary hand of providence which seemed always to reach out over Bob at St Andres showed itself. On the 19th he was on the green in two, but Tolley, chipping, laid

Left No luck for Britain. Roger Wethered congratulates Bob Jones, the opposing captain, after America's victory, 10 to 2, in the 1930 Walker Cup
Above Bob Jones moves a step nearer the Grand Slam when he collects the US Open Champion-ship at Interlachen, Minneapolis, 1930. Here (arrowed) he chips to the 9th green, his fairway shot having, some spectators said, bounced off two lily-pads on the guarding lake

Leo Diegel in action during the 1930 British Open at Hoylake. His curious putting action, with elbows pointing out sideways, became known as 'diegeling'. Three years later, in the Open at St Andrews, Diegel needed one putt to win and two to tie. He completely missed his second putt!

Right Johnny Revolta, who won the USPGA tournament in 1935 and twice played in the Ryder Cup. He was one of the most successful players in the 1930s on the professional tour
Below right The trophy for winning the US Masters at Augusta

himself a dead stymie. He failed to negotiate it and Jones, with two putts, won the match. (It was instances such as these which finally disbarred the stymie from the game in 1951.)

Even in the sixth round, Jones was a narrow winner against 'Jimmy' Johnston, the 1929 US Amateur Champion. In the semi-final, his opponent George Voigt, also American, found himself two up with five to play, but on the 14th, with a cut tee-shot and a strong wind blowing from left to right, he drove out of bounds. One down and four to play Bob Jones won – but it was close. In the final over 36 holes against Roger Wethered, the Englishman began to show strain and was missing several tiny putts. It was all over on the 30th green. The 15,000 crowd, admirers of Jones to a man, burst on to the course and caused a near riot. So Bob had won the one major title that had previously eluded him.

In comparison, he had no trouble in the Open at Hoylake, though his play was not half so confident and he had taken 5 shots to get down from 12 yards at the 8th hole. He simply plugged on and won by guts, instinct and 2 strokes from Mac Smith and Leo Diegel. He was fêted down Broadway with a ticker-tape welcome, a speech of congratulation by Mayor Walker and a dinner at the Vanderbilt Hotel.

Next appointment, the US Open at Interlachen, Minneapolis, early June. It was blazing hot, over 100 °F on the course and humid, and after the first two rounds Horton Smith was leading with 142. Harry Cooper and Jones were tied at 144 and Mac Smith trailed one behind. In the second round Jones had played the famous Lily Pad shot, when his ball skipped three times on the surface of the water before hopping up on to the bank of the lake. In the final round, Bob took three 5s and his success depended on playing a good final hole. He did, sinking a 40-foot putt for a birdie. Mac Smith finished with a fine 70, but had to be content as runner-up, 2 strokes behind.

So in the year at whose beginning that great-hearted little Scot Bobby Cruickshank had said: 'He's simply too good. He'll go to Britain and win the Amateur and the Open and then he'll come back over here and win the Open and Amateur. He is playing too well to be stopped this year' – Bob Jones was one success away from this prediction. Merion, two months after he had won the US Open and six years after he had won his first Amateur, was the scene destined for the final leg of 'The Grand Slam'. He qualified on a Tuesday with a record-equalling 142. On

Above Bob Jones inspires a cavalry charge up the side of a bunker during the 1930 Walker Cup match at Royal St George's, Sandwich, England
Right A fine example of good footwork and balance as Horton Smith drives during the 1930 British Open at Hoylake

Wednesday he beat the Canadian champion Ross Somerville 5 and 4 and beat another Canadian, Fred Holblitzee, in the afternoon, again 5 and 4. One of his greatest dangers was George Von Elm, but he had fallen in the second round after an incredible *10* extra holes against Maurice McCarthy Jr. Thursday no trouble, and Friday saw a poor Jess Sweetser beaten 9 and 8. On Saturday, with a brisk breeze sweeping the Merion Cricket Club course, his final opponent was the nervous, thin Gene Homans. It was an anticlimax. Some 18,000 spectators watched Jones, 8 up and 8 to play on the 29th tee, on in two with his opponent, but Homans's putt was not good enough and Bob had achieved the most amazing feat of all time. The crowd applauded the achievement, but not particularly that last match. Jones had achieved all he could.

The year 1931 saw the introduction in the United States of what was to be a provisional ball: a ball no smaller than 1.68in. and no heavier than 1.55oz. The next year saw the last of this balloon ball; it was no good; and in the States the new ball was to be 1.68in. minimum diameter and 1.62oz maximum weight, the specifications it still has today.

The depression was also making its presence felt. Miniature golf courses, needing only a putter and a ball to play, flourished and declined. Tournaments reduced purse money. Some fell completely by the wayside. Bob Jones decided to retire from tournament golf.

Above Gene Sarazen strikes one of the 286 strokes that won him his second US Open title at Fresh Meadow Country Club, New York, 1932, the year he also won the British Open

Right The 'Silver Scot', Tommy Armour, American Open (1927), British Open (1931), Canadian Open (1927, 1930, 1934), French Open (1920) and USPGA (1930) champion. Born in

He was twenty-eight. He had won all he wanted, the strain was great, his law practice suffered, as did his privacy, and he was relentlessly pursued by admirers of all ages who did little to alleviate the tension of trying always to please them – knowing that failure was terrible disappointment for his devoted fans.

But his loss – plus the effects of the depression – hit golf badly. Jones, on the other hand, had a full life to look forward to and he succeeded in a remarkable way. He had always, while playing tournament golf, stuck to his amateur status, despite the most tempting blandishments. But now with golf before the public behind him, he was willing to accept some very useful offers. He became a broadcaster, with his 'Boswell', O. B. Keeler, and made two series of films, for $180,000. They were very good. And then Augusta . . . but more of that later.

Golf became unpredictable and perhaps a little ragged after Jones's retirement. And it is a good time to consider three players whose names have cropped up but to whom I have not yet given their fair due. Macdonald Smith was a very great golfer, but the major championships never fell into his lap. His successes, like Leo Diegel's and Harry Cooper's, were on all the other tournaments. The three of them did very well financially, but not one of them took the US or the British Open. One of the hardest tasks in writing this book is to do justice to those who were genuinely great but who never quite captured the public's attention because they never scaled the so-called heights. (I beg to be forgiven for perhaps a hundred golfers whom I have only mentioned in passing or whom I have omitted on the grounds of comparatively limited space.)

Mac Smith had been twenty when he tied for the US Open in 1910 with his elder brother Alex and Johnny McDermott. But in the play-off he shot a 77 to Alex's 71 and Johnny's 75, and that was the nearest he came until Interlachen in 1930. Nine times Mac Smith was within three strokes of the winner of the

Scotland in 1895, he left for the States in 1922 and became one of the finest teachers the game has known. Here he is shown driving in the early 1930s

US or the British Open, but he had a tendency to crack when all seemed within his grasp. He was a beautiful golfer, with a perfect temperament, and yet something always held him back in the great events. A native of Carnoustie, he went to America and had thoroughly absorbed the spirit of his adopted country. But one of his most typically tragic experiences was at Prestwick in the British Open in 1925 when, as Henry Longhurst has written: 'If Mary Tudor had the word Calais engraved upon her heart, so assuredly must Macdonald Smith, who died after the recent [Second World] war, have had Prestwick. Colossal crowds turned out . . . to see the Scotsman win. In their combined determination to see the play at all costs . . . and to cheer their hero home, they lost him the ambition of a lifetime and, as I shall always feel, set permanently in the top of the second-class a golfer to whom no heights might have been unattainable.' On his last round, hustled by his adoring fellow countrymen, he slumped to

Above left Craig Wood, who did the 'double' by winning the US Masters and US Open in 1941. In the 1933 British Open at St Andrews he drove into the bunkers in front of the 5th green, a distance of 430 yards! Here he is driving from the 7th tee at Southport, England, during the 1933 Ryder Cup
Above Densmore Shute in action during the 1933 Ryder Cup match at Southport, Lancashire. Watching is Abe Mitchell, one of his opponents in the foursomes. The Britons won 6 to 5, their last win until 1957

Above Gene Sarazen competing for the US Open title at Oakmont, 1935. Sam Snead once compared putting on Oakmont's greens to 'trying to stop a ball half-way down a flight of marble stairs'

an 82. The stewarding of the vast crowds had broken down completely, and the hordes just trampled uncontrolled all over the course.

Leo Diegel adopted an extraordinary hunched putting style, with his elbows sticking outwards, his forearms parallel with the ground and his forehead almost touching the top of his club. He hit his other shots flat footed, with a noticeable snatch on his backswing, but he played beautifully, so all his contemporaries thought. Bernard Darwin thought him 'in a way the greatest golfing genius I have ever seen'. But it all seemed to start early. After three rounds in the 1920 US Open at Inverness, Toledo, he was a stroke behind the leader, Vardon. The fourth round was going well, when a spectator coughed at the top of the (jerked) backswing. On his next shot there came the most infuriating of all interruptions – a friend came to tell him of something that had happened to Ted Ray. Diegel was exasperated. He had to be content to tie with Vardon, Jock Hutchison

and Jack Burke as runner-up. He did well many times in both the US and British Opens, but never well enough. He did, however, stop Hagen's run of wins in the PGA championship. The Haig had won in 1921 and from 1924 to 1927, but in 1928, when Diegel took his third Canadian Open he also defeated the field in the PGA, beating Al Espinosa 6 and 5 at Five Farms, Baltimore. On his way to victory he had defeated Tony Manero, George Christ, Hagen and Sarazen. He kept his title in 1929, beating Johnny Farrell 6 and 4 at Hillcrest, Los Angeles. He was runner-up, with Mac Smith, to Bob Jones in the British Open in 1930 and seemed to have the British Open in his grasp at St Andrews in 1933, but his worrying, electrically charged temperament failed him over the last four holes.

Harry Cooper was an Englishman reared in Texas, where his father was a professional. Like Diegel, 'Light Horse Harry' would rush after all his shots, hardly able to wait to play them, but unlike Diegel he had a much sunnier

The American team sets sail on the *Manhattan* in preparation for their defence of the Ryder Cup in 1937. Back row: left to right, Horton Smith, Byron Nelson, Sam Snead, Johnny Revolta; centre row: Gene Sarazen, Densmore Shute, Ralph Guldahl, Tony Manero, Henry Picard, and Fred Corcoran; kneeling: Ed Dudley and George Jacobus. Corcoran was team manager, Jacobus President of the USPGA

time the stewards called me to the 1st tee I had severe stomach cramps. I am told I looked pretty green and certainly my 40 out did not improve my confidence. Coming home I began with three 5s and had three long holes to come. The crowd anticipated the most appalling 'blow-up' in championship golf. I continued to struggle and feared a fourth consecutive 5 at the 13th, but blessedly I holed a 10-footer for a 4. The tension relaxed and I played as I had been playing all week, returning a 79 for a total of 283, equalling Gene Sarazen's record at Prince's in 1932. But I had missed a short one on the 18th and would otherwise have broken the record. It was a marred victory, but it was a victory, and for the first time since Arthur Havers's triumph the British Open trophy was back where it belonged, and by 5 shots after all.

I remember at the Royal St George's Golf Club the enormous encouragement that the old brigade gave me. James Braid, J. H. Taylor and Ted Ray always seemed to be there to egg me on and Harry Vardon, now hardly able to walk, accompanied by his life-long friend Arthur Brown, would sit at the 'Maiden' and watch us pass. Harry was ill on the last day, and I took the Cup, that he had so gloriously won six times, to his bedroom, where we both unashamedly wept. And a word too for Henry Longhurst's gentlemanly loan of his camel-hair overcoat, which I wore over my pullover for the presentation ceremony. My jacket was in my car, which I used as a changing room as usual, for the clubhouse was out of bounds then for professionals.

The next year the British Open was at Muirfield. I played a beautiful opening 17 holes, but took 6 at the 18th. My 68 was still a course record for the altered course, but I was despondent. Alfred Perry won that year, playing nerveless golf and beating Alfred Padgham by 4 strokes. 1935 was also the second year in which Lawson Little won both the US and British Amateur titles. He had been a member of the US Walker Cup team

in 1934 at the age of twenty-four and 1935 was his last year as an amateur. He tied for fourth place in the Open at Muirfield and then in 1936 turned professional, winning the Canadian Open 8 strokes in front of Jimmy Thompson. He won the US Open in 1940 in a play-off against Gene Sarazen and will always be remembered as one of the first really long hitters who could control the ball perfectly.

The year 1936 was Padgham's. He had won the *News of the World* Tournament in 1930, had a wonderfully placid temperament, huge hands, and, in 1936, perfect putting won him the British Open Championship at Hoylake. He held his club with an unbelievably light grip and played with an upright three-quarter swing, quite different from his nearest opponent in that Open, James Adams, whose flowing swing and magnificent putting kept him in the match until the last hole. In the same year the USPGA limited the number of clubs a player could carry to fourteen. (Lawson Little had needed a powerful man as a caddie, for his huge bag contained twenty-six clubs! This was overdoing things.)

In 1937 I won the British, German and Czechoslovakian Opens and managed to defeat Denny Shute, who was then the reigning PGA champion, in a £500 ($2000) match at Walton Heath, England. The British Open was held at Carnoustie in Scotland. Great Britain had been soundly beaten by the visiting American Ryder Cup team and their presence in the Islands meant even stronger than usual opposition from the other side of the Atlantic in the Open. Carnoustie is a very long course, over 7000 yards, with penal bunkers placed just where a reasonable drive might pitch, and the weather over that rather rough course was diabolical on the last day. I had played reasonably in the week, taking 74, 72 and 73, while Reggie Whitcombe, the youngest of those three remarkable brothers, was leading the field three up on me (72, 70 and 74). In the last round, played in continuous heavy rain, pools on the course enlarging to small ponds, with no hope of

keeping body or club-grip dry, Reggie managed 76 and the cameramen crowded round him as the new champion. Henry Longhurst has called my last round of 71 'the greatest single round of golf I ever saw'. I myself would certainly say it was one of the best rounds of my career, only one outside the course record then. I had to get a 4 on the last hole to equal the record. I decided to try and carry the burn and not play safe short of the water. My no. 2-iron shot finished in a sand bunker, hole-high to the right of the green. I played out safely from the hard wet sand with my ordinary niblick short of the pin and got down in two putts. I would not risk my broad-soled sand iron in case the club skidded on the hard sand and the ball might fly out of bounds, which was just beyond the green on my line of play. I had

won, 2 strokes ahead of Reggie, but without the record.

The British Amateurs had their first win in the Walker Cup at St Andrews in 1938 and Ralph Guldahl won the US Open for the second successive time, only the fourth golfer to achieve this feat. He also won the Western Open for the third consecutive time and was runner-up in The Masters, as he had been the year before. Ralph had beaten Sam Snead in the Open in 1937 and these were certainly his years. He was not a beautiful player to watch. His swing was rather upright and he kept his left heel firmly on the ground throughout, but the puzzling thing in his game was that he allowed his club to slide about in his right hand, rather like Alfred Perry, Dai Rees, Bobby Locke and the Whitcombes. Though in the years 1932–40 he won many champion-

Above Byron Nelson stays down on a recovery from a sand-trap on the 1st hole of the play-off, on the way to winning the US Open Championship at Philadelphia, 1939
Right Bobby Locke of South Africa, on one of his early visits to Britain, with the 'Law' in attendance
Overleaf At some courses you even find bunkers in the middle of the green. Here Ben Hogan splashes out in the 1948 US Open, Los Angeles. This is Riviera's famous 'island' sand-trap and Hogan went on to win in 276 strokes, beating the old record for the course by 5 strokes

ships, including the Masters and the Canadian Open (for the second time) in 1939, he suddenly lost his form and faded out of tournament golf.

Several fine golfers were making their names known as World War II approached. Sam Snead and Jimmy Demaret, who had won the Texas PGA five times in succession by 1938, were new names in the headlines. Bobby Locke had been sweeping up every title in sight in South Africa since 1935 and by 1939 had added the Irish, New Zealand and Dutch Opens to his tally. Byron Nelson won the Masters in 1937 and the US Open in 1939 and Ben Hogan was beginning to show the promise of his amazing post-war record.

Demaret was the supreme showman both on and off the course. His first big tournament win was the Masters in 1940 and this was when the thirty-year-old Texan first leapt into international prominence. He was to win another two Masters, but these were after the war. Very popular with the spectators, his war service with the US Navy kept him out of tournament golf until 1945. Bobby Locke, or to give him his full name, Arthur D'Arcy Locke, became a professional in 1938 and won the South African Open in 1935, 1937, 1938, 1939 and 1940 and the South African Amateur in 1935 and 1937, before joining the South African Air Force.

Byron Nelson began his golfing career with Ben Hogan as a caddie at Fort Worth, Texas, and having won the Masters in 1937 he went on in 1939 to win the US Open, the Western Open, the North and South Open, the Vardon Trophy and was runner-up in the PGA Championship – perhaps the finest golfing achievement since Bob Jones's 1930 Grand Slam. By 1940 he was the second highest money winner and also beat Sam Snead one up in the PGA Championship. In 1942 he secured the Masters for the second time, beating off his old associate Ben Hogan, and by 1944 he was the leading money winner, with a record amount of $37,967.69 in war bonds. In 1945, when golfers were beginning to return from the war, Byron Nelson played

in thirty-one out of thirty-eight tournaments, won seventeen and was runner-up in seven. It was a shame that Nelson's great years coincided with the war years when so many of the greatest competitors were away fighting. Nelson was one of a group of tough Texans – Ben Hogan, Lloyd Mangrum, Demaret and Jug McSpaden, joined by the Virginian hillbilly, Sam Snead – who captivated the golf enthusiasts during those lean years. There was a friendly rivalry between Nelson and Hogan, so close in age and upbringing, but Nelson, exempted from military service through hemophilia, never had a chance at the height of his powers to take on Hogan in a challenge match, so the argument raged among their respective partisans. Nelson's play was dull. The 'mechanical man' had neither Snead's flair nor Hogan's amazing grim tenacity. His shots seldom went wrong, but they were seldom sensational. While Nelson's opponents were unavoidably away, he and his friend McSpaden (who because of a sinus condition had also been rejected from service) played through the worst years, 1944–5, with government encouragement to boost morale at home while the fighting continued in Europe, Africa and the East. In the year of his record money winnings, Byron scored an average 69.67 for 85 rounds, and if you are a statistics fan that is a pretty remarkable average. He was voted 'Athlete of the Year' by the Associated Press. In his phenomenal run of eleven tournament victories in 1945 he was eventually stopped at Memphis by a fine amateur, Freddie Haas, but he still beat all records, with an average of 68.33 over 120 rounds (!) and total earnings of $52,511. Again he was voted 'Athlete of the Year'. Ben Hogan would occasionally appear during the war years in his lieutenant's uniform to oil the springs of his golf. His and Nelson's was a ding-dong confrontation. In 1945, Hogan beat Byron by 3 strokes at Richland with a 19-under-par 265. Nelson won at Spokane. Hogan beat him with a record 261 at Portland and a fortnight later at Seattle 'Lord' Byron hit 62, 68, 63 and 64 – 259 –

In 1945 Byron Nelson set a world record of 259 for 72 holes in the Seattle Open. It stood for more than 20 years, Mike Souchak beating it with 257 in the 1955 Texas Open

with Ben Hogan trailing 20 shots behind. But the pace of golf was too hot for Nelson's physique, and a chronic stomach illness forced him to retire soon afterwards to his cattle 'ranch' in Texas, which he claims does not make any money. It is only 90 acres, but he loves running it almost single-handed when he is not acting as TV commentator for the ABC chain in the USA.

Ben Hogan's form really came to a peak after the war, but before I turn to the post-war years, when international golf began to open itself out to British Commonwealth, European Continental and Far Eastern players, it is worth remembering that by 1941 Hogan had twice taken the Vardon Trophy. Another player who must be left for the next chapter is Lloyd Mangrum, who had the honour of winning the first of the resumed US Open Championships in 1946.

The war years were comparatively sparse for golf. The only important events that I have not covered were Lawson Little's 1940 victory over Gene Sarazen in the US Open at Canterbury and Craig Wood's double in 1941 when he won both the US Open and the Masters, defeating Denny Shute in the Open by 3 strokes and Byron Nelson at Augusta by the same margin.

5 The Post-War Years: 1946 to today

IN MY EARLY YEARS as a professional golfer, travel round the world was slow. With the rapid expansion of civilian air travel after World War II it became extremely fast and it was soon no real problem to play on two different continents within a week. At the same time television gave millions of people a greater opportunity to watch sports, and commercial interests increased earnings for professional sportsmen by leaps and bounds so that even for the less talented performers there were pickings which were attractive enough to swell the professional ranks. As a result, it is not only the winners of the classic tournaments whose names become part of the household equipment. With golfers, young and old, the good, and the not so good, are all exposed to millions of words from journalistic pens or to the searching cameras of the television film crews. The 'greats' are still outstanding, but many others are known who snatch a title one day and fade for the rest of the year, or who quietly make their way round one of the smaller circuits – players to be reckoned with, especially in terms of money winnings, but players whose numbers are so great that only the largest and most comprehensive encyclopedia could do justice to them.

Therefore by and large I must concentrate on the 'greats' and on the major tournaments. There are many players I have played with, or watched or coached, whom I would like to include, but space and the dangers of compiling merely a confusing list of names forbid it.

The year 1946 was the one when golf picked itself out of the war slump. Only in Germany, Italy and Japan of the pre-war golfing countries did it have to wait for a later renaissance. Italy was the first of these three to resume its Open, in 1947, followed by Japan in 1950 and Germany in 1951. But both the United States and Britain reinstated their Opens in 1946 and got off to splendid starts. Lloyd Mangrum, with his trim moustache and glossy black hair parted down the centre, had been a professional since

Sam Snead about to sink a long putt on the last green for a birdie 3 to tie Lew Worsham for the 1947 US Open at St Louis, Missouri. Worsham won the play-off by a stroke, 69 against 70

1929, as a teenager. The pre-war years had not been successful, apart from some circuit wins in the States and becoming runner-up to Jimmy Demaret in the 1941 Masters. But after the War, in which he had served and been wounded, he became one of the biggest money winners. He was a Texan, of much the same age as Ben Hogan, Harold McSpaden, Byron Nelson and Jimmy Demaret, and in the 1946 Open, at Canterbury, Cleveland, he became the first US Open winner after the war, beating Byron Nelson and the big Vic Ghezzi in a 36-hole play-off. He went on later in the year to defeat Ghezzi yet again in the Argentinian Open. Byron Nelson had had an unfortunate experience on the 16th green in the third round of this US Open, when his caddie accidentally kicked his ball. Nelson had to accept a penalty stroke and three-putted on the 17th green. Not long after, he retired from competitive golf. One of golf's greatest 'machines' had gone into cold storage.

But there were two golfers whose day was still to come – Ben Hogan and Sam Snead – and a 'Colonial', Bobby Locke, was to break open the smugness that had infected American professionals. Ben Hogan was, perhaps, the most dedicated golfer ever to drive a ball off the tee. As I wrote in 1948: 'Hogan is a serious, likeable person with an intense capacity for concentration, and an appetite for practising which exceeded all previous standards by its ardour and duration . . . When they say Hogan is a "killer" – they really mean it, for he is as tough a golfer as ever trod a links.' By the early 1940s he was leading the money winners (1941 and 1942) and again he led in 1946, with $42,556.16 and in that year he won his first major title – the National PGA at Portland, Oregon. Phenomenally strong, he loathed losing. He was small (135lbs), uncommunicative, unsmiling. He aimed for the pin and hit the ball a long way and very straight but at that time with a big draw. In 1948 he won his first US Open over the long (7200-yard) Riviera, Los Angeles, course. He beat Jimmy Demaret by 2 strokes, and also won other tournaments,

Left Norman von Nida, one of
Australia's finest golfers, winner
of the Australian Open in 1950,
1952 and 1953, and subsequently
a most respected teacher
Right Some 'body English' by
Cary Middlecoff at the third extra
hole of a play-off with Lloyd
Mangrum for the Motor City
Open title, Detroit, 1949. Still
level after 11 extra holes they
agreed to tie

Flory Van Donck, of Belgium, who dominated Continental golf after World War II. Altogether he won 18 Open Championships on the Continent and was twice runner-up in the British Open. Here he is playing his tee shot at the 12th in the Spalding Tournament, Moor Park, England 1954

including his second PGA and the Western Open and picked up the Vardon Trophy. He was again the leading money maker. His score of 276 in the Open was a record. He added three more Opens – in 1950, 1951 and 1953 – but these were verging on miracles.

In 1949, 2 February, Hogan and his wife Valerie, were involved in an appalling car accident when in fog on the way home to Fort Worth they hit a bus head on. Hogan threw himself across his wife to protect her and for his bravery received a broken left ankle, a double fracture of the pelvis, a broken collar-bone and a smashed rib. In hospital he suffered a thrombosis and, like ex-President Nixon, an abdominal operation involved the tying off of the main arteries to his legs. His life was saved but his golf seemed a thing of the past. And yet the accident seemed to strengthen his resolve to win. His attitude mellowed, but his competitive spirit became even keener. Every hole was a challenge to his tiring and damaged legs. The man of whom someone once said: 'He looks at you like a landlord asking for next month's rent', sharpened his game but blunted his taciturnity. He had been on his back for nearly two months after the crash. His recovery was slow but determined. By January 1950 news flashed through the sports columns that he had entered the Los Angeles Open. As he trudged round on weakening legs he shot a 73, a 69 and another 69. Sam Snead beat him in the play-off, but 'the Little Man' was back. After that his career was literally incredible – the Open in 1950, the Masters and the Open in 1951 and again in 1953, coupled with the British Open. He was runner-up to Sam Snead in the Masters in 1954 and to Jack Fleck in the 1955 US Open. He had started the 1953 British Open at Carnoustie in cold, stormy weather, 3 strokes behind Frank Stranahan. The second round put him 2 strokes behind the Britishers, Dai Rees and Eric Brown, and his third round put him level with Roberto De Vicenzo. His closing round of 68 (a total of 282) sealed his victory. The four tying runners-up were Frank Stranahan,

125

Left Frank Stranahan, then an amateur, plays to the short 16th during the 1953 British Open at Carnoustie. He finished in a tie for second place with Dai Rees, Peter Thomson and Antonio Cerda, 4 strokes behind Ben Hogan. He turned professional in 1954. Watching (left) is the Sudanese player, Hassan Hassanein, winner of the French Open Championship in 1951 and Egyptian Open champion 1949-52
Right Bobby Locke sinks another putt on his way to winning the 1957 British Open at St Andrews. It was to be his fourth victory. Note his curious 'round-the-corner' putting style

Dai Rees, the formidable Peter Thomson, from Australia and the Argentinian Antonio de Cerda – 7 strokes behind. Hogan could be ranked at this time with Harry Vardon and Bob Jones as one of the top three all time greats.

Sam Snead is a totally different person. The sweetest swinger of a club that has ever been seen, his one sadness is that he has never won the US Open. He has won the Masters three times, the PGA three times and the British Open once. This incredible player, now sixty-three years old, still plays first-class golf, even if he no longer carries away the major trophies. Like Gene Sarazen and Roberto De Vicenzo he is still one of the biggest draws at a tournament and there is an enormous aesthetic pleasure to be gained simply from seeing that fluid, flawless, smooth, strong swing. With his inevitable brimmed hat – to hide his bald head – and his treasure-house of

earthy stories, his continued good humour, despite his greatest disappointment and, though it has been overworked, his outgoing hillbilly character, Sam is the greatest fun to be with and his continued presence on the courses has given golf one of its many strands of continuity. His putting has always been considered his weak point – indeed he now putts 'side-saddle', the two hands wide apart. He hits consistently very straight and very long indeed, and, perhaps like myself, if he gets the ball on the green in fewer shots than others, it is not surprising that his putting average is not so good as those who take an extra shot through the green and then put their ball closer to the pin for a chip and one putt.

In 1937 Ralph Guldahl beat Sam in the US Open by 2 strokes. In 1939, at Philadelphia, Sam only needed a 5 to win. He took an 8. In 1947 he lost to Lew Worsham at St Louis,

in the play-off. This was a crushing blow. Sam had holed a curling 18-foot putt to tie Lew with a score of 282. In the 18-hole play-off they were all square at the final hole. Both played their balls to within three feet of the hole. Sam walked to his to knock it in when Lew Worsham halted him. 'Just a minute,' he said, 'what makes you think you're away? Perhaps I am.' Sam said that he was entitled to finish once he had started putting. In fact, when the referee measured the distances, Sam's ball was a half-inch further from the hole. Upset, Sam missed his putt – and lost. He was runner-up to Cary Middlecoff in 1949 and to Ben Hogan in 1953. 'Slammin'' Sammy has won more than a hundred and thirty tournaments. He was leading the 1963 Masters with four holes to play, but his putting did him a disservice. Today he uses his unorthodox 'side-saddle' technique, which seems to have steadied his one possible weak-

Left 'Do you remember?' George Duncan (left) and J. H. Taylor recall the past during the Teachers' Seniors' Championship at Fulwell, England, 1957. 'J.H.' was then in his 87th year. He died in 1963, George Duncan in 1964 *Above* Henry Cotton with Bob Jones, Augusta, 1957. 'R.T.J.Jr.' was by then confined to a wheel-chair. He died in 1972

Gary Player (left) on an early visit to England, 1957. With him are Trevor Wilkes (centre) and Bobby Locke

ness and which has got rid of the 'yips' or 'twitch' which haunted him and made putting an effective torture.

Arthur D'Arcy (Bobby) Locke was not a beautiful player to watch, but he knew his natural hook and he was a great short game and putting expert – perhaps the greatest ever. His characteristic knickerbockers and open attitude at first endeared him to Americans when he hit the continent in 1947, but unfortunately his realization of the pickings to be made resulted in an attitude towards winning which spoiled his natural temperament. He had won everything to be won in South Africa by the time he was seventeen, in 1935. He was well known in Britain by the time he made his 1947 assault on the States. He had beaten Sam Snead in South Africa, where he was born, in twelve out of the sixteen matches they had played. His first engagement in America was the Masters, where Americans had a good look at the mature twenty-nine-year-old, who had flown on more than a hundred Liberator missions during the war. His score of 289 over four rounds of the Augusta course was presentable, but it seemed to offer no real challenge to the leaders. Jimmy Demaret won, for the second time, with 283, after a play-off against Byron Nelson and Frank Stranahan. Frank Stranahan's performance was particularly remarkable, for it was the first time an amateur had come near to winning this prestigious event. But after the Masters Locke's pace hotted up. He won four out of the next five tournaments he played in and by the end of the year he had won seven, and was second in the money-winning list. For the first time since Vardon and Ray's tour, an outsider had shown the American professionals that they were beatable. He also reminded the public that golf was not the most earnest game in the world.

Jimmy Demaret had managed to keep a flicker of friendly contact with the spectators, but for the rest of the professionals each round seemed to be a grim struggle where every distraction was some sort of crime. Bobby Locke was relaxed, would smile at the crowds and appeared to enjoy himself. The $20,000 he won in 1947 determined him to return the following year. By mid-summer, 1948, he had already won a further $20,000, putting him on the same earnings level as Ben Hogan and Jimmy Demaret. In 1949 he turned his attention to the British Open at Sandwich, which he won with a record-tying score of 283. He kept his title the next year with a new British Open record of 279 at Troon, 4 strokes better than the previous record which was held by Locke himself, Gene Sarazen, Harry Bradshaw and myself. At Old Troon he was level with Dai Rees and Roberto De Vicenzo at the end of the third round. De Vicenzo, putting wonderfully, came home with 281 and Locke, who was playing behind him, knew his target exactly. On the last hole he needed a 5 to win, but characteristically holed out for an easy 4, to leave De Vicenzo runner-up and Dai Rees and Fred Daly tied for third place. He won the British Open again in 1952 at St Anne's, and in 1957 at St Andrews became the eighth man to win the historic Open four times, beating the Australian, Peter Thomson by 3 strokes and tying his own record of 279. Perhaps, to give some idea of Bobby Locke's success in his best years, we might look at his wins from 1950 to 1952:

1950 British Open, South Africa Open, South Africa Professional, Transvaal Open, Dunlop Tournament, Spalding Tournament, All-America Open, North British Tournament

1951 South Africa Open, Transvaal Open, South Africa Professional

1952 British Open, French Open, Mexican Open, Lotus Tournament

In 1948 I won my third British Open, though 1947 at Hoylake had been a disappointment

The grief of a champion. Gary Player, his wife at his side, sheds a silent tear over the 6 he took at the last hole during the 1959 British Open at Muirfield. He thought it had cost him the title. Instead he won by 2 strokes

Top left Arnold Palmer gets the ball clear of the rough by the 14th fairway on his way to winning the 1961 British Open at Royal Birkdale. This was the first of his two consecutive British Open victories
Left Jack Nicklaus on his first visit as a professional to Britain. Here he is driving during the Piccadilly tournament at Hillside, 1961

Above Astonishing crowd scenes round the 18th green at Troon, 1962, as Arnold Palmer nears his second successive British Open Championship. His total of 276 was a record, equalled 12 years later by Tom Weiskopf on the same course

for me. But fortunately for Britain Fred Daly had won, and a worthy champion he proved to be, for he also won the *News of the World* PGA Championship in the same year. I had been seriously ill and, indeed, at the end of the war I had to take a year's enforced convalescence. I was weak and decided that before trying for the 1948 British Open I needed rebuilding, so I went, with the encouragement of my good friend Ed Lowery and others, to America in the spring, where with good food I soon built up my strength and confidence. Back at Muirfield for the Open I played well, set up a course record of 66 on the second round, and led Fred Daly by 5 strokes. Alas, since 1948 the British Open has only twice gone to British players – in 1951 to Max Faulkner and in 1969 to Tony Jacklin.

Post-war British golf saw two Irishmen consolidating their positions. Jimmy Bruen had played brilliantly at the age of eighteen in the practice rounds before the 1938 Walker Cup. Though his play was not quite so outstanding during the match itself – he halved a foursome (playing with Harry G. Bentley against John W. Fischer and Charles Kocsis) and lost his singles against Charles Yates – he was nevertheless in a team which beat America by 7 to 4, which compared very well with the 1936 Walker Cup match when America whitewashed the British team 9–0. In the first Amateur Championship in Britain after the war, where the British had their initial sight of Frank Stranahan, Jimmy Bruen struggled a bit through the early rounds, but in the final, after a shaky morning, he used all his power and completely shattered his Anglo-American opponent Robert Sweeney.

The other Irishman was Fred Daly from Balmoral, Belfast. After Sam Snead's victory over Bobby Locke in the British Open in 1946, Fred Daly took the Open at Hoylake in 1947. Defeating R. W. Horne and Frank Stranahan, he beat me later in the year in the

News of the World Tournament (the Professional Match Play Championship) at St Anne's. We met in the semi-final and Daly played a stream of magnificent shots and I had to give up on the 16th green, having suffered three dead stymies in the last seven holes. Daly went on to beat Flory van Donck, one of the best players to have come from Europe (in his case Belgium). Fred Daly had become the first man since James Braid to win both the Open and the Match Play Championships in the same year. Fred, who was a great match play exponent, won the *News of the World* Tournament again in the following year. This was an astonishing feat, only previously achieved by Abe Mitchell.

It was also in 1948 that Roberto De Vicenzo, one of the game's great perennials, first appeared, with hardly a word of English, in Britain. He played impressively in the Open, but he had to wait until Hoylake, 1967, before he captured the coveted trophy, though he was runner-up to Bobby Locke at Troon in 1950. Today he is still playing a fine game and his charm makes this Argentinian one of the most popular of players with the crowds.

Cary Middlecoff and Frank Stranahan, an altogether brasher figure and son of a wealthy industrialist, were two of a bunch of post-war American amateurs who could show the professionals that they were beatable. Stranahan was a mechanically sound golfer with a magnificent natural physique. He had been coached by Byron Nelson, but he at first lacked the social graces which the gentle game of golf demands, and had twice offended British crowds by boorish behaviour. On his second attempt at the British Amateur at Carnoustie in 1947 Frank was playing a Scot, George Morgan, when on the first green of the third-round match Morgan, holing for a four, conceded Stranahan's half by knocking the American's ball back to him. Stranahan quite unnecessarily and in fact, by the rule book, wrongly argued that he had in effect only played three strokes, and had therefore won the hole. The hole was ruled halved and

Frank's churlish behaviour was enough to put the spectators thoroughly out of sympathy with him. However, he behaved impeccably later in the year at the British Open and went on the following year to win the British Amateur, a feat he repeated in 1950. He was runner-up in 1952. He never quite managed to pocket the American Amateur. Despite his great wealth he turned professional in 1954, and had a reasonable career on the circuit.

Middlecoff, as a twenty-three-year-old dental lieutenant, had been the first amateur ever to win the North and South Open, at Pinehurst in 1945. He went on to win the US Open in 1949 (the year that Ben Hogan was recovering from his accident), one stroke ahead of Clayton Heafner and Sam Snead, and he repeated this win in 1956, this time one stroke ahead of Ben Hogan and Julius Boros, a great and unobtrusive player, son of a Hungarian immigrant, who had won the US Open in 1952. Not long afterwards, Boros won the World's Championship. This tournament started in 1943 and took place at Tam O'Shanter in Chicago. It was launched by George S. May, a wealthy businessman, and boasted the largest purse in golf. It was still the richest tournament in 1953 when Lew Worsham scored an eagle at the last hole. Chandler Harper had sunk his ball for a birdie 3. With 279 on his score card for the four rounds he seemed assured of the first prize of $25,000 and also a number of $1000 exhibition matches. Behind him were the last threesome – Dave Douglas, Doug Ford and Lew Worsham. Worsham, while Harper was being congratulated, knew he needed a birdie to tie for the play-off. His drive ended 104 yards from the green. A simple wedge shot dropped the ball short of the pin and it rolled gently into the cup. Chandler Harper had been defeated by one stroke and Lew picked up the $25,000 prize money and subsequently played in thirty-seven $1000 exhibition matches for George S. May. His eagle had netted him $62,000! The World's Championship was later scrapped by May as

a result of arguments with the PGA.

In Britain a tall and colourful professional, Max Faulkner, temporarily regained the British Open trophy for his home country in 1951 at Portrush. It was the first time the Open had been played in Ireland. Bobby Locke had won the last two Opens and clearly intended to win again. Frank Stranahan was rarin' to go, and no one had any illusions about how good Tony Cerda could be. A promising Australian, Peter Thomson, had come over with Norman Von Nida, and so, although the field was not of the strongest, it was formidable enough. In the event, by the beginning of the final round, Locke, who had not been feeling well, was trailing Faulkner by 8 strokes, and Cerda, the little Argentinian, by 6. As luck would have it (bad or good depending on your viewpoint), Cerda, who was playing magnificently, pulled a shot very close to the out-of-bounds fence on the 16th, the Stables. It meant a 6 for the hole. Nevertheless, he finished only 2 strokes behind Faulkner. Next year, 1952, Bobby Locke won again and in 1953 the trophy went to Ben Hogan, who played almost faultless golf at Carnoustie, in Angus, one of the toughest courses in the world. Hogan was dubbed 'the wee ice mon'.

Peter Thomson had been runner-up to Bobby Locke in 1952, and with the Welshman Dai Rees, Frank Stranahan and Tony Cerda had repeated this feat in the Open in 1953. Then started a quite remarkable run of British Open victories. Not so well known in the States as in the Commonwealth, partly because of his dislike of the 'big' ball, Peter Thomson was and is a very fine player. He is best on fast, unwatered courses and has studiously avoided the flashier (and more lucrative) side of modern professional golf. Yet in the 1950s he virtually made the British Open his own. Poor organization and even poorer prize money had scrubbed some of the gilt off the Open's pre-eminence among championships, and America had not fallen over herself to contest the title. However, this does not rub any of the glory off Peter Thomson's record of runner-up in 1952 and

1953; winner in 1954, 1955, 1956; runner-up in 1957; winner in 1958 and 1965.

Despite the lack of world interest in the British Open for the moment international golf, helped by television and larger purses, was bouncing ahead. John Jay Hopkins, president of General Dynamics Corporation, had in the early 1950s concocted a truly international tournament, abetted by Fred Corcoran, the former tournament director of the American PGA. The newly formed International Golf Association held its first championship at Beaconsfield Golf Club, Montreal, in 1953. Eight countries, sending two-man teams, arrived – Argentina, Australia, Canada, England and South Africa combined, Germany, Mexico, and the United States. Much to the United States' chagrin it was the Argentinians who captured both possible trophies. Tony Cerda won the individual International Trophy, while he and Roberto De Vicenzo won the team Canada Cup. The United States came fifth. In the following year at Laval-sur-le-Lac, close by Montreal, the match was played over 72 holes, double that of the first year. Twenty-five countries sent their two-man teams. Again the United States was disappointed. The Australians, Peter Thomson and Kel Nagle, won the Cup, and Canada's Stan Leonard, who had been the 1953 runner-up for the individual prize, this time won it.

Again the Argentinian team did well, coming second in the Canada Cup. The United States rose to third place. Today the trophy is known as the World Cup (as is the World Amateur Golf Team Championship for what was formerly called the Eisenhower Trophy).

The German Open of 1953 was won by Flory van Donck, a great Belgian golfer, whose presence dominated European continental players in the years from 1935 to the mid-1960s. Five times Belgian Open champion, twice German Open champion, five times Dutch Open champion, three times French Open champion, the Portuguese Open champion in 1955 and twice the Swiss Open champion, he also played every year for

Years take their toll of the nerves. Sam Snead's 'side-winder' putting stroke on the 8th green, during the Teachers' Seniors' Championship at Wallasey, Cheshire, England, in 1967
Overleaf Tony Lema uses his iron during the 1965 Ryder Cup at Southport, England

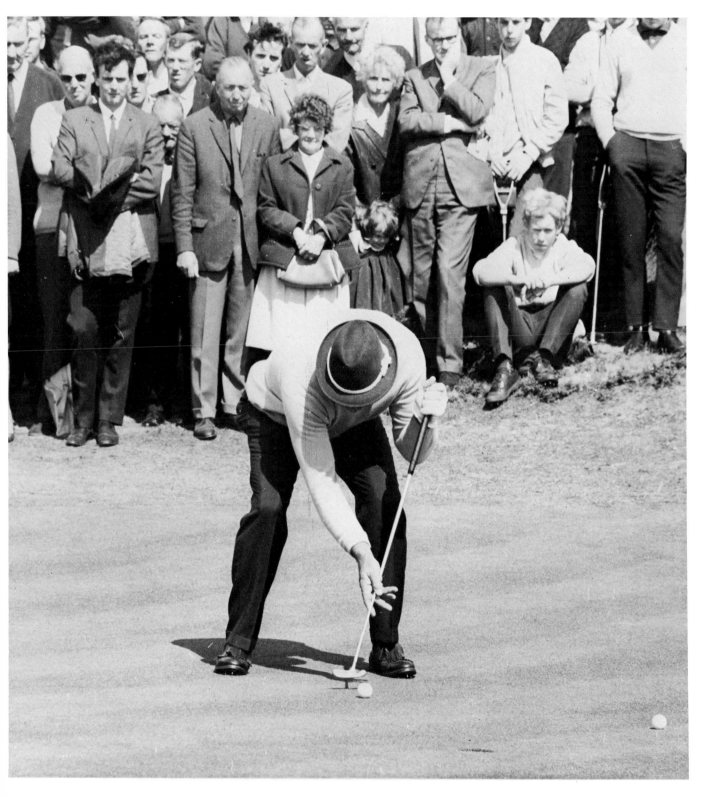

Above Jack Nicklaus gets a ruling and a copy of the local rules during a Piccadilly World Match-Play Tournament. After this incident at the 9th hole, the referee, Col. Tony Duncan, withdrew his services and his place was taken by Gerald Micklem, English Amateur champion in 1947 and 1953

Near right Bob Dickson, well muffled against the cold, urges on a putt during the 1967 Walker Cup match at Royal St George's, England. The same year he won both the British and US Amateur Championships. The only other amateurs to have performed this feat were Harold Hilton (1911), Bob Jones (1930) and Lawson Little (1934 and 1935)

Far right Tony Jacklin during his early days on the American circuit, here in the Greater Jacksonville Open, Florida, 1968. He won it, becoming the first British golfer for many years to win an American tournament

Belgium in the Canada (World) Cup from 1954 to 1964. He was also runner-up in the British Open Championship in 1956 and 1959.

The early 1950s brought to the fore a young, fair-haired, smooth swinger, Gene Littler. After his win in the US Amateur in 1953 it was thought that a new star had been born. In the following year he was in the lead in the US Open, having turned professional, but a botched 8-foot putt on the last hole gave the event to Ed Furgol. The Open was played at Baltusrol and was the first US Open to be televised nationally, but even more remarkable was the winner. Ed Furgol, who was then thirty-seven years old, was an unknown. A childhood injury had left him with a withered left arm, bent at the elbow and eight inches shorter than his right. Though he played in the Ryder Cup in 1957, he never

achieved anything remotely comparable to his 1954 US Open victory. ('Unknowns' also won the US Open in 1955 – Jack Fleck defeating Ben Hogan in a play-off – and 1969 – Orville Moody, who had been a sergeant in the US Army, in which he had served for fourteen years, including a spell in Korea, where he had won their Open three times.)

Gene Littler never quite endorsed his early promise. For some years after the 1954 US Open his swing deserted him and although he won this coveted championship in 1961 his only other successes in top-class tournaments were limited. In 1969 he was runner-up to the left-handed New Zealander Bob Charles in the Piccadilly World Match Play Tournament at Wentworth, Surrey, England, and shortly after underwent major surgery for cancer. That he came back, his swing as

Above The ever-popular Arnold Palmer well protected from too enthusiastic fans
Left and right Contrasting seaside courses. The 1967 Walker Cup is in progress at Royal St George's, Sandwich (left), a traditional British link, while the fine course at Shinnecock Hills, Long Island, (right) reflects a more artificial course architecture

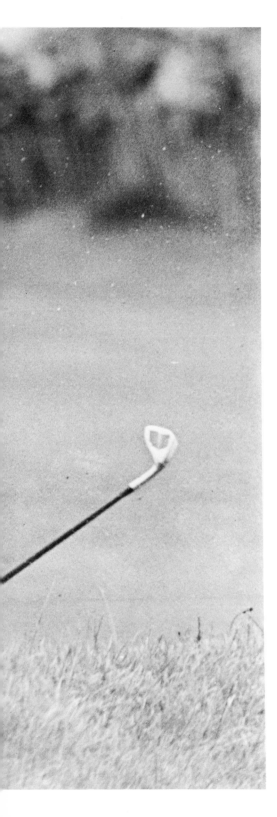

Gary Player had no need to look anxious. He had long since proved himself the greatest bunker player in the world. This shows him at the British Open at Carnoustie, 1968—which he won

flawlessly simple as ever, is one of the marvels of the seventies.

If Gene Littler's star faded, one newcomer in 1954 was to prove the biggest 'draw' that the game of golf has ever seen. Arnold Palmer was the son of a professional in Latrobe, Pennsylvania. His victory in the US Amateur at the Country Club of Detroit that year was not seen at the time as being of particular significance. He defeated Robert Sweeny by one hole – the championship having been played by match-play from its birth in 1893 until 1965 when, because of the huge entry, it became a stroke-play event. The experiment did not last long. By 1973 the United States Golf Association had reverted to match-play, considering this form of golf to be more in keeping with the traditions of the game. That same year, 1954, Palmer turned professional. He was twenty-five years old and in the 1960s, along with Gary Player and Jack Nicklaus, became part of a modern 'Triumvirate'.

Player first came to world-wide notice in 1956 when he finished fourth in the British Open at Hoylake. He finished five strokes behind Peter Thomson, who thus secured his third consecutive victory. Gary Jim Player was born in Johannesburg towards the end of 1935 and to confirm his arrival as a world-class golfer he defeated Bobby Locke in 1957 over 108 holes. Though Locke was to win that year the British Open for the fourth and last time, a new South African ruler was in power. A man whose whole life has been devoted to his family, his religion and his golf, Player's hours of practice are prodigious. A strict non-smoker and non-drinker (both of which pleasures he dismisses as detrimental to peak physical condition) he goes to extremes to achieve the acme of bodily fitness by exercise and of golf perfection by practice. Probably no one in the history of golf, with the possible exception of Ben Hogan, has so completely given himself to winning the game. So ascetic an approach has naturally attracted undue publicity but he has always been a courteous and honest player, attri-

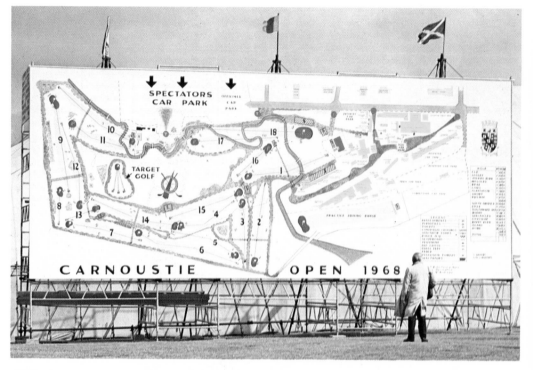

butes that have made him popular on international courses. The simple gesture of acknowledging the applause of the crowd with a quick touch of his inevitable cap has never appeared to his followers to be more than a modest appreciation of the public's warm feelings towards one of the most consistently forceful practitioners.

By 1958 Palmer was poised to break most records with his shattering game. He had won one big championship, the 1955 Canadian Open but now, at Augusta, he was about to take the Masters, his first major title. On the 13th hole in the final round he struck not only the vital blow, but a stroke that epitomized his whole glittering career. His second shot, a three-wood over the water, came down 18 feet from the pin and he holed the putt for an eagle 3. He won by a stroke.

The attendance at Augusta that year was estimated at 25,000. All through his playing career Palmer's magnetic personality has attracted huge crowds and 'Arnie's Army', as his fervent followers were christened, became not only an effective fan club but

Above Organization for major tournaments becomes more and more efficient. This huge diagrammatic map of the Carnoustie course gives spectators all the information they need
Right Jack Nicklaus plays an awkward shot from a bunker on the 2nd hole during the 1969 Ryder Cup match at Royal Birkdale, England. The result was a draw

also something of a menace. Since their enthusiasm for Arnold was unabated, even when he was losing, special precautions had to be taken to protect the game of other players. There were times when he even putted last, to keep the gallery still while others holed out. The great year was 1960, when Palmer's golf was supreme and the world realized that here was one of the finest sporting personalities of all time. Indeed he came to be elected Athlete of the Decade.

At that Augusta, Ken Venturi, with a score of 283, seemed assured of victory in the Masters and he even went to try on the green jacket of the champion and to be briefed for television interviews. But Palmer was still prowling the course. He needed a birdie at either the 17th or 18th to tie and the general opinion was that these two punishing holes would be too much for him. A putt of 25 feet for a 3 at the 17th gave him the birdie he needed. Now, however, Palmer stood the chance of winning outright and he went all out for another at the 18th – a massive drive into the wind, a low 6-iron stroke five feet from the hole and then a putt that wavered on the edge before dropping to give him a famous victory. He had won the Masters for a second time and did so again both in 1962 and 1964, a record since equalled only by Nicklaus.

That finish was typical of Palmer's play. An immensely powerful man, though subsequently outdistanced by the even stronger Nicklaus, much of the lure he has provided for the public has been in these amazing spurts when his position seemed irrecoverable. I doubt whether any other golfer ever managed to gather in such astonishing clutches of birdies when they were needed most.

Palmer's imagination was now fired. 'My ambition is to win the Masters, the US and British Opens and the PGA all in a single year,' he said. 'I think it would be a greater achievement than Bobby Jones's Grand Slam in 1930.' It certainly fired the imagination of Arnie's Army. Vast crowds of all ages,

Above left Jean Garaialde provides a model example of keeping the head still on the 14th tee during the 1969 Piccadilly World Match-Play Tournament, Wentworth. One of France's finest

players, his first French Open
victory was in 1969
Above 'Don't touch it, it might
sting.' Gary Player (left) and Bob
Charles examine a wasp during
the 1968 Piccadilly World Match-
Play Tournament. Player won it,
but Bob Charles was to win it in
1969, breaking the monopoly
held by Palmer and Player since
the Tournament started

Left Tony Jacklin strikes out towards the club house at St Andrews from the 18th tee during the 1970 British Open. With him is Lee Trevino. Jack Nicklaus was the winner, but Trevino took the title in 1971 and 1972

Above Gary Player seeks gold again from under a rainbow at the Piccadilly World Match-Play Tournament

Right Billy Casper about to chip during the 1970 Alcan Tournament

151

some knowing little about golf, turned out to watch him at the US Open at Cherry Hills in Denver. And how they were rewarded. Palmer was 7 strokes behind the leader, Mike Souchak, by the end of the third round but the magic was there. On the final round he immediately picked up four birdies in a row, got his par at the 5th, birdied the 6th and 7th, dropped a stroke at the 8th and got his par at the 9th. He was out in 30, played the last nine holes in one under par and, with an aggregate of 280, had won again. There was, however, a cloud on the horizon. Only 2 strokes behind was an amateur. His name was Jack Nicklaus.

The third leg of Palmer's Grand Slam took place at St Andrews, the obvious venue for the centenary of the British Open. Here he again made one of his surging rallies but rain postponed the last round and it washed away his momentum. The winner was instead that fine Australian, Kel Nagle, who edged out Palmer by a stroke. So the dream was unattainable. In the PGA at Akron, Ohio, Palmer led after the first round but he slumped again and the title went to Jay Hebert.

Palmer's first disappointment at the British Open was amply rewarded in the following two years, for he won both at Royal Birkdale in 1961 and Troon in 1962. His appearance – and success – at the somewhat declining British Open did more than anything else to bring that most venerable of championships right back into the mainstream of golfing classics, as it were, alongside the Masters, US Open and PGA. After all if 'the Charger', as he was christened, felt it worth competing for, then surely any lesser golfer from the United States could hardly be blamed for having a go. Palmer was the first golfer whose winnings exceeded one million dollars. All over the world his businesses thrived. Apart from endorsing sports equipment and cars and many other pieces of merchandise, he wrote books, acted, taught and became a tycoon of immense vigour and responsibilities. His golf undoubtedly suffered from

Above 'That's it, then.' Tony Jacklin (right centre) and Brian Barnes (left centre) examines a waterlogged 14th green during the 1970 British Open at St Andrews. A violent storm halted play for the day in the first round, Jacklin, the defending champion, having just played the first nine holes in 29

152

Above Doug Sanders' wife buries her face in her hands as her husband misses a short putt on the last green which would have given him the 1970 British Open at St Andrews. The following day Jack Nicklaus beat him in the play-off

Right Doug Sanders cannot believe it, but there his ball is, still above ground after he had missed the putt that would have won him the 1970 British Open

Left Jack Nicklaus, the 'Golden Bear', leaps for joy during the 1970 British Open Championship at St Andrews, which he won, after a play-off with Doug Sanders. This was his second and consecutive win
Top right Tony Jacklin assesses the lie of the land as he measures up for a putt in the Piccadilly World Match-Play Tournament at Wentworth, England
Below right Max Faulkner, with Henry Cotton and Tony Jacklin the only British player to have won the British Open since World War II. Here, at the age of 54, he competes in the 1970 British Open Championship

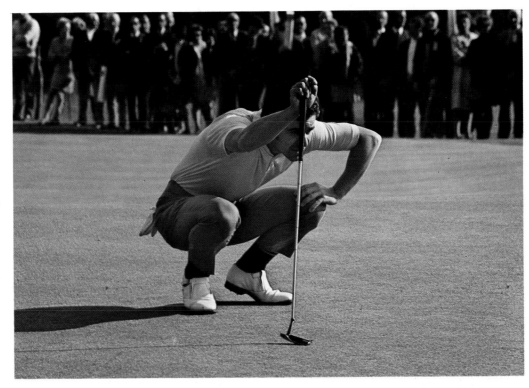

these extraneous, though profitable, activities, but he always maintained golf came first.

Player's rise to the very top in international golf coincided closely with that of Palmer though, as the younger man by seven years, he lasted longer. The little South African won his first 'big one' – the British Open – at Muirfield in 1959 and then added to it the Masters in 1961, Palmer for once blowing up with a double bogey 6 at the last hole. A year later Palmer got his own back. It was, however, a close thing, the two tying over 72 holes but Arnold, trailing by 3 strokes in the play-off, picked up five birdies in seven holes from the 10th and won by 3 strokes.

There were other fine golfers around, of course, notably Dow Finsterwald, a consistent top money winner, and also Billy Casper. A Mormon, Casper won the US Open in both 1959 and 1966. In his first success, at Winged Foot, he needed only 114 putts for the 72 holes, a phenomenal performance on some of the most difficult greens in America. But increasing weight worried him and he lost

40lbs by going on an extreme diet. It changed his whole appearance but not his golf. He remained among the leading money winners of all time and in 1970 won the Masters. Golf in the sixties enjoyed its greatest boom and it was on to this floodlit stage that Jack Nicklaus strode.

Nicklaus was nineteen in 1959 when he first won the US Amateur Championship. Two years later he won it again and at once he turned professional. His play cannot be described as stylish but at his best he hits the ball further and straighter than anyone. He has never quite had the same grip on the crowds as Palmer in his heyday but for a number of years it was difficult for him. Palmer was everybody's hero and could do no wrong. It is immensely to his credit that by good manners, and at times unsurpassed golf, Nicklaus in the end came to be both loved and respected almost as much.

He can be infuriatingly slow, especially on

Above Miller Barber, a consistent player on the American professional circuit, backed by the scaffolding of the stands at Carnoustie, the scene of the 1968 British Open Championship

Right Lee Trevino, in a typically dramatic pose, sinks to his knees. A most unorthodox stylist, he has constantly amazed by brilliant play during apparent slumps

159

the greens. Every shot is calculated with cold precision. Courses are measured meticulously before each tournament, landmarks noted. Nothing that can possibly improve the accuracy of his game is omitted. He possesses too an excellent temperament and is rarely ruffled. Off the course he is charming and amusing and over the years has become one of the most knowledgeable authorities on all the many facets of the game.

Nicklaus first upset Arnie's Army by beating their hero in a play-off in the US Open at Oakmont in 1962. It was his first victory as a professional and the following year he took the Masters. A bothersome hip injury prevented him from defending the American Open a few months later and a 6, 6 finish at Royal Lytham lost him the British Open. However, within a few more weeks he had collected the PGA at Dallas and, by winning three of the major championships in less than two years, had announced himself as one of the greatest golfers of all time. By 1973, when he won the PGA for a third time, he had exceeded Bob Jones's record of thirteen major championships.

Palmer did not win a major tournament in 1963, nor Nicklaus in 1964, yet in the two respective years they were each time the leading money winner. In 1965, however, Nicklaus took his second Masters, due to an extraordinary third round. He, Player and Palmer were level after 36 holes, but on a perfect day Nicklaus nonchalantly holed the course in 64, equalling Lloyd Mangrum's record for Augusta, set in 1940, and subsequently matched again in 1974 by a British player, Maurice Bembridge. Nicklaus's last round of 69 gave him an aggregate of 271 for the 72 holes, 3 strokes inside Ben Hogan's 1953 record.

The year 1964 was notable for Palmer's fourth Masters and Ken Venturi's only American Open. It came from the most unlikely circumstances at the Congressional Club, Washington, Venturi suffering agonizingly from the intense heat and in the midst of a playing slump that had lasted three years.

Top left Roberto DeVicenzo, back at the US Masters in 1972, scene of his greatest tragedy in 1968. Argentina's finest golfer, and one of the most popular players, he has won more than 20 Open Championships
Below left A familiar sight at Royal Birkdale in 1971, Liang Huan-Lu from Taiwan, much better known as 'Mr Lu', raises his blue hat to the crowds during the British Open. He was runner-up in this Championship to Lee Trevino
Above Golfers perform all sorts of contortions when long putts fall. Mind you, this by Lee Trevino did win him $30,000 in the Doral Eastern Open at Miami

So bad was his condition after a third round of 66 that a doctor had to be called to pass him fit for the last round. Even then he played the course as if in a daze. Instinct got him round in 70 and he won by 4 strokes from Tommy Jacobs.

In 1966 Nicklaus won his first British Open, at Muirfield, a course he came to love as much as any in the world. A year later Roberto De Vicenzo, that gifted Argentinian, beat him at Hoylake. Here was a most popular victory and within twelve months De Vicenzo was within a pencil lead of adding to it the Masters. It was perhaps the most tragic 'miss' of all time.

Through the eyes of television virtually the whole world watched him hole for a birdie 3 at the 17th and, on his forty-fifth birthday, earn a tie and a play-off with Bob Goalby on 277 after a final round of 66. But in the excitement of the moment Vicenzo looked only at the total on his card, for which the player is not responsible. He failed to look closely enough at the figures for each hole, failed

consequently to notice the four – not the three – at the 17th and had to accept therefore the 67 to which his score added up. Goalby, Tommy Aaron (who had marked the card) and every official tried all they could to find a loophole so that justice could be done. The rules allow no escape.

That same year the near-bankrupt son of a Mexican gravedigger popped up out of the ground as it were to win the American Open at Oak Hill, Rochester. He had a peculiar scything swing and most people said it was a fluke. But his name was Lee Trevino and he proved everybody wrong by regaining the title in 1971, winning the British Open back to back in 1971–2 and taking the PGA in 1973. His alert mind and quick wit made him an instant favourite with the galleries but it sometimes concealed a rare and natural golfing talent.

If the golfing development was all outwardly in the American shop-window, progress was being made elsewhere too. The Miguel brothers, Sebastian and Angel, hauled

in a collection of continental titles; Ramon Sota, likewise a Spaniard, followed their example; Jean Garaialde became the most famous French golfer since Arnaud Massy; Flory Van Donck became something of an ageless Belgian wonder; and Roberto Bernardini came from Italy to win the Swiss Open in successive years. Just also as Palmer had lit the golfing fire in the States, so was Tony Jacklin to do the same in Britain.

No British player had won their native championship since Max Faulkner in 1951. But at Royal Lytham in 1969 Jacklin opened the doors to let the sunshine in again when, with a remarkable display of bunker shots, he held off a challenge by Bob Charles, the world's leading left-hander and winner of the British Open six years earlier.

Top left Gary Player in contemplative mood at the Piccadilly World Match-Play Tournament, Wentworth, England
Below left Tom Weiskopf, one of America's finer younger players, and victor in the 1973 British Open Championship
Right Gary Player, lifts his caddie for a sight of the green during the 1972 British Open at Muirfield

Left Peter Oosterhuis (6ft 5in) makes himself as small as possible as he studies the line of a putt during the Martini International Golf Tournament at Abridge, England (1972), a course designed by Henry Cotton *Above* Coming up the finishing straight as spectators rush for a good vantage point during the 1972 Dunlop Masters Tournament at Gosforth Park, Newcastle, England, won by Bob Charles. The reason for the charge was 'Jacklin fever', though in fact it was Peter Oosterhuis who made the best British showing, finishing runner-up

That last drive at Lytham is threatened by a line of diagonal bunkers but, with the British Isles holding its breath as one man, Jacklin's tee shot boomed over the lot to the very centre of the fairway. His 7-iron second found the very middle of the green and at once he was engulfed by the stampeding hordes, losing temporarily a shoe but emerging smiling and, within the year, adding to the British title that of America as well. He was the first Briton to win the US Open since Ted Ray in 1920.

Jacklin won by 7 strokes at Hazeltine, the biggest margin since Jim Barnes's 9-shot victory in 1921. At 7151 yards, this was the second longest course ever to be used for the US Open, but though strong winds blew throughout, Jacklin spreadeagled the field, 2 strokes ahead after the first round, 3 after the second and 4 after the third. Dave Hill, the runner-up, sourly commented that Hazeltine was a good place for cattle.

Britain also possessed the finest amateur golfer in the world in Michael Bonallack. In 1970 he won the British Amateur Championship for the third year in a row and the fifth time in all. At home, if not abroad, he won everything it was possible to win time and time again. A marvellous putter, he was one of the greatest amateurs of all time. Few records can stand comparison.

In 1970 the British Open was held at St

Above The young Mormon star, Johnny Miller, blasts out on to the green during the 1973 Piccadilly World Match-Play Tournament. Top money winner in 1974, he started 1975 with a string of wins and galvanized a slightly faded Nicklaus into competitive spirit again
Right Tommy Aaron, during the 1973 Ryder Cup. This was the year when he won the US Masters, where, back in 1968, he had unfortunately wrongly marked Roberto DeVincenzo's card

Top left Laura Baugh playing in the 1974 Colgate Ladies' Open. She was the US Ladies' Champion in 1971 and, born in 1955, the youngest winner since Beatrix Hoyt in 1896
Below left Martha Kirouac blasts out of a sand-trap during the 1972 Curtis Cup match, won 9 to 7 by the United States. Born Martha Wilkinson, she was the 1970 US Ladies' champion
Above Judy Rankin, joint runner-up in the 1972 US Women's Open Championship, putts during the 1974 Colgate Ladies' Open

Andrews, and Jacklin, holder now of both Opens, went out in 29 in the first round. At the 14th, the lead his almost certainly, a terrible storm broke and play was suspended until the following morning because of flooding. The magic left Jacklin that night and the title went to Nicklaus, though it will be remembered as much for the putt that Doug Sanders missed on the last green for outright victory. Nicklaus did not give him a second chance in the play-off and had achieved another landmark – victory at the home of golf.

Two years later Nicklaus was within sight of the world's four major championships in a year. He won the Masters and then, on fiendishly slippery greens, added to it the US Open at Pebble Beach. Muirfield, his great love, lay as the third hurdle and he arrived a week early to prepare. Not until too late, a glorious final round of 66, did he move into top gear and Trevino beat him to the line.

The little Mexican had thus won the British Open in successive years, during which time he had also collected the American and Canadian Opens. Both times in Britain he stepped virtually off the trans-Atlantic flight to show everyone else the way round, a feat

Above Fifty years after his first appearance in the British Open, Gene Sarazen (right) came back to Troon in 1973 to have another go. Here he chats to Arthur Havers, the 1923 champion. The following day, Sarazen, at the age of 71, holed the 8th in one, a nostalgically popular feat
Right Maurice Bembridge playing in the Portuguese Open at Penina in 1973. The year after at Augusta he equalled the course record with a 64 in the last round in the US Masters. Penina is one of two courses designed in Portugal by Henry Cotton and it is where he himself lives. In the background is the luxury Penina Golf Hotel

Left Arnold Palmer, a legend in his own lifetime, during the 1973 Ryder Cup at Muirfield, Scotland. Palmer was beaten 4 and 2 by Peter Oosterhuis in the singles on the last day, but the United States won overall 19 to 13
Above Peter Oosterhuis (left) and Tony Jacklin rehearsing a dance routine! Or perhaps they were just watching somebody else putt (1974)
Right Hale Irwin, US Open and Masters champion, 1974

previously performed by Tony Lema in 1964. Lema's death in an air crash in 1966 was an enormous blow to the game, for he possessed great gifts as a golfer, as he showed in confounding a typical St Andrews gale. Like Trevino in subsequent years, one practice round was enough. Yet at Muirfield in 1972 Trevino had luck on his side as well. He three times chipped in and once holed out from a bunker. His par 5 at the 71st hole, where he sank his ball from off the green, whereas Jacklin 3-putted for a 6, was one of the most dramatic late swings in championship golf.

Golf was exploding, too, in the Far East and Japan. Lu Liang Huan, otherwise known as 'Mr Lu', from Taiwan, endeared himself to all by finishing runner-up to Trevino at Royal Birkdale in 1971, won the French Open the same year and, with Hsieh Min-Nam, took the World Cup the following year. 'Jumbo' Ozaki began also to do for Japan what Palmer and Jacklin had done for their respective countries. Golf was now very much a world game.

After a comparative spell in the shadows, Player came back too, to win the PGA in 1972. Two years later he took both the Masters, for the second time, and the British Open, for the third. Though thirty-eight, and some said beyond his best, his 1974 victory at Lytham typified his tenacity. He led the field for all four rounds, a colourful black caddie, 'Rabbit' Dyer, at his side. Four strokes behind came a rising British player, Peter Oosterhuis.

But the balance of power was shifting nonetheless. Johnny Miller played a brilliant last round of 63 to win the 1973 US Open at Oakmont and shattered all records with nine victories on the American circuit twelve months later. Then there was Tom Weiskopf taking the 1973 British Open at Troon, though Gene Sarazen's hole in one at the Postage Stamp 8th at the age of 71 was something that will perhaps be remembered even longer.

Who will be the next stars? We inevitably look towards the many young Americans but

Gary Player about to win his third British Open Championship. But he has to play left-handed with his putter after over-shooting the 18th green at Royal Lytham in 1974

it could equally happen that one of the excellent Japanese players will win a major championship. So many events are played on so many circuits through the world that it is hard to assess future potential. The Australian Graham Marsh has had great success on the Far East circuit and is still comparatively unknown in the West. Oosterhuis is tipped to repeat Jacklin's great achievements. The ever-increasing number of tournaments, while it gives lesser players their chance of brief glory, also sadly means that timetables are tight, so that the big names are able less and less to assemble frequently because of the clash of dates. But this marvellous game is always one of total fascination and surprise, and I look forward to seeing the young, many of whom I have coached, battling it out with the established heroes.

b Women in Golf

I HAVE SAID VERY LITTLE about women golfers. This is not only ungallant but it is not even a reflection of my admiration for them. In an earlier book, *This Game of Golf*, I chose the English amateur Joyce Wethered (now Lady Heathcoat-Amory) as 'The Best Player Ever?'. That was in 1948. I have no reason to change anything that I wrote about her then. Yet, as in so many other sports, it has been the men who have – perhaps too often – stolen the limelight.

We know that Mary Queen of Scots was playing some form of golf in the fields beside Seton in 1567 but it is not until the eighteenth century that we have any further reference to women playing, this time at Musselburgh, where the fisherwomen appear to have relaxed with a golf club.

The first ladies' golf club was founded in 1867 at St Andrew's, Scotland. The Westward Ho! Ladies' Club in England was formed in the following year and then followed a string of new clubs as the popularity of the game spread among the ladies. In France, the home of many fine women players, Pau was founded in 1874. In the early days of these clubs it is almost certain that only the putting greens were used and the only club to be wielded was

the putter. But in June 1893 the first British Ladies' Championship was held over 9 holes of Lytham and St Anne's Club, on the Lancashire coast. Ladies' courses were then separate from the men's and remained so for a very long time. The holes were short and by modern standards easy. The card for that first championship at Lytham and St Anne's shows lengths of 244, 221, 328, 182, 207, 337, 120, 272 and 221 yards. The quality of play was poor and surprisingly not one Scot was competing. By far the greatest of those who did compete was Lady Margaret Scott, the winner, who beat Miss Issette Pearson by 7 and 5, but her total of 41 strokes for the first nine holes (the championship was played over two rounds of the course) was not very remarkable. (Her brother, the Hon. Michael Scott, won the British Amateur in 1933, at the age of fifty-five, the oldest man ever to win the trophy.)

However, the ladies were on the golfing map and the biggest spur to their ambitions was the formation, shortly before that first British Ladies' Championship, of the Ladies' Golf Union. This was inaugurated on 19 April 1893. The driving force behind it was Miss Issette Pearson and other members of the

Royal Wimbledon Club, ably assisted by Dr W. Laidlaw Purves, of the same club. The aims of the Union were simple: to promote the interests of the game; to obtain uniformity of rules; to establish uniform handicapping; to act as arbitrators over points of uncertainty; to arrange the Annual Championship Competition and to obtain the necessary funds. Lady Margaret Scott was to win the first three Ladies' Championships, but then gave up competitive golf. Others, later, showed that the ladies' game was as good, if not as long, as the men's. Today the LGU performs the same function as well as arranging international matches.

In the United States the first Ladies' Championship took place in November 1895 at Meadowbrook Club, Hempstead, New York. It was decided by stroke play and the winner was Mrs Charles S. Brown. No one could possibly say that the score was im-

pressive. The last six holes of her first nine were 4, 5, 7, 9, 14 and 6. However, the breakthrough for women had been made, and although it was some time before professionalism crept in, the early women players had made another inroad into the spheres traditionally preserved for men. The liberation of the sporting woman had advanced a step. After this initial year of stroke play, the championship in the United States changed to match play – as it has been ever since.

The year after Mrs Brown's victory, the US Ladies' Championship was won by a teenager, Beatrix Hoyt, only sixteen years old. She, like Lady Margaret, won for three successive years, and then in 1900 gave up tournament golf. At about the same time, two sisters, Harriott and Margaret Curtis were making their names. 'Peggy' Curtis was a superb brassie player, who could hit the ball with this club further than many men. She

Above Early days on the Knokke links, Belgium
Right Cecil Leitch takes a rest during the French Ladies' Championship at Le Touquet in 1920. Miss Leitch brought a new dimension to women's golf, particularly with her iron play. She was British Ladies' champion four times—1914, 1920, 1921, 1926 and French Ladies' Open champion 1912, 1914, 1920, 1921 and 1924

Overleaf Mrs Bowles, playing in
the 1921 Ladies' Parliamentary
golf match at Ranelagh, London,
was obviously the possessor of a
powerful swing

was the runner-up in the US Ladies' Championship in 1900 and 1905 and won it in 1907 (defeating Harriot), in 1911 and 1912. Her last championship was in 1949, when she was sixty-nine. Her two-years-older sister Harriot won the Championship in 1906. For women's golf the Curtis sisters were all-important. They had come to Britain for the British Ladies' Championship in 1905, when it was held at Cromer in Norfolk and when an unofficial match was first played between the ladies of the two countries. Much later, in 1930, an unofficial match between the American and the British ladies at Sunningdale in Berkshire created such interest that the sisters donated a trophy and in 1932 the first Curtis Cup match took place. The setting was Wentworth in Surrey, and the British team, though they fielded a side which included Joyce Wethered, Enid Wilson, Wanda Morgan and Molly Gourlay, were far too casual. The Americans won by five matches to three. In those early days the match consisted of three 36-hole foursomes and six 36-hole singles, but in 1964 the formula was changed to three 18-hole foursomes and six 18-hole singles. Since the first match the Cup has been competed for every other year, except for the war years. It was resumed in 1948. Britain did not win a match until 1952.

In her own Ladies' Championships, Britain was supreme at home until 1927, when a great French golfer (Mademoiselle Simone Thion de la Chaume) wrested the title from its native isles. Later she married René Lacoste, the tennis player, and their daughter, Catherine, later became a golfing champion. The British ladies lost again in 1928, this time to another Frenchwoman, Mademoiselle Manette Le Blan, but not until the amazing 'Babe' Zaharias won at Gullane in East Lothian, Scotland, in 1947, did the Americans win. The British Ladies' Championship has always been a match-play championship and

Glenna Collett (Mrs Vare), six times US Ladies' champion, limbers up before her match (which she lost) with Joyce Wethered during the British Ladies' Championship at Troon, 1925. One of the greatest of American women golfers, her 6 wins in the US Ladies' Championship remain a record

Sylvia Marshall, runner-up in the
British Ladies' Championship,
1928, congratulates her victor,
Manette le Blan of France

since 1913 has been played over 36 holes. It is, of course, a purely amateur tournament.

In the early years of the twentieth century the standards of women's golf rapidly improved. Dorothy Campbell won both the British and the US Ladies' Championships in 1909, and went on to win the British again in 1911 and the US in 1910 and 1924. She had been born a Scot but later married an American named Hurd and her last American victory was played under American citizenship. In 1910, one of Britain's greatest lady golfers, Cecilia (Cecil) Leitch, defeated Harold Hilton in a 72-hole handicap match at Walton Heath and Sunningdale in England. Receiving 9 strokes a round, she won by 2 and 1. Cecil Leitch had first attracted notice when the LGU visited St Andrews in 1908. She was seventeen years old, and Enid Wilson has written that she 'struck the ball with a crispness and ferocity that was a revelation to all who saw her reach the semi-final at her first appearance in the British'. Her iron shots were particularly powerful. She became the British Ladies' Champion in 1914 and after the First World War went on to win again in 1920, 1921 and 1926. She was twice runner-up (in 1922 and 1925), both times to Joyce Wethered. The United States, out of the war except for 1917 and 1918, had an equally impressive player in Alexa Stirling (Mrs Alexa Stirling Fraser), Bob Jones's lifelong friend, who won the US Ladies' Championship in 1916, 1919 and 1920, and was runner-up in 1921, 1923 and 1925. But the real excitement of the 1920s was the competition between Cecil Leitch and Joyce Wethered. Miss Leitch was playing in the English Ladies' Championship in 1920 at Sheringham, in Norfolk. She reached the final easily, and there seemed no reason why she should not win. But her opponent happened to be a tall, pale young lady from Surrey, in southern England, Joyce Wethered. By the third hole of the second round, Miss Leitch was 6 up and 16 to play and her position, as was to be expected, seemed impregnable, but Miss Wethered, inexperienced though she was, produced a

run of threes and went on to win by 2 and
1. So started the career of a golfer of whom
Bob Jones said: 'I have not played golf with
anyone, man or woman, amateur or professional, who made me feel so utterly
outclassed.'

These two players were very different in
style and temperament – Miss Leitch, with a
flat, ungraceful swing and a vital outgoing
personality, and Miss Wethered with a fluid
swing and a frailer physique and retiring
personality. Their continued rivalry through
the 1920s did a great deal for women's golf
and was watched with increasing fascination.
Joyce Wethered won the British Ladies'
Championship in 1922, 1924, 1925 and 1929.
She was the English Ladies' Champion from
1920 to 1925. One more informal event that
she made famous was the Worplesdon Mixed
Foursomes. This is played annually on a
pleasant heathy course in Surrey. It started in
1921, when Joyce Wethered and her brother
Roger were defeated, but after that Miss
Wethered won no fewer than eight times,
making her last appearance, with her husband,
in 1948, when they were beaten in the final.

In America, Miss Glenna Collett had
annihilated most opponents in 1924 and
crossed the Atlantic in spring 1925 to challenge
Miss Wethered. The British golfer proved too
good for her on that occasion, but the
American's play had alerted Britain to the
new transatlantic threat. Miss Collett (Mrs
Edwin H. Vare) never captured the British
Ladies' Championship, but she was twice
runner-up (in 1929 and 1930), beaten by
Joyce Wethered and then Diana Fishwick
(Mrs A. C. Critchley), but she won the US
Ladies' a record six times – in 1922, 1925,
1928, 1929, 1930 and 1935. Her chief com-
petition in the States came from Alexa
Stirling, Edith Cummings, Marion Hollins,
Maureen Orcutt, Miriam Burns, Virginia Van
Wie, Mary K. Browne and Helen Hicks. In
the 1930s some of these players were still
prominent in America, while the younger
Patty Berg and Betty Jameson came to the
front before the war. In Britain Enid Wilson

Diana Fishwick (Mrs Critchley) at
Sunningdale in 1930. She was
playing for the United Kingdom
against the United States in the
international fixture that two
years later became the Curtis Cup.
In this same year she became
British Ladies' Champion. She
was also French Ladies' champion in 1932 and Dutch Ladies'
champion in 1946

Left Diana Fishwick, then 19 years old, is carried shoulder high from the 18th green at Formby after defeating the great American champion, Glenna Collett, 4 and 3 in the British Ladies' Championship, 1930
Below left Joyce Wethered, her brother Roger and (right) Cyril Tolley at the finale to the British amateur season, the Worplesdon Mixed Foursomes, in 1933. Both Joyce and Roger Wethered had played (and were defeated in the final) at the first of these events in 1921. Altogether, with various partners, Joyce Wethered won this event eight times
Right Henry Cotton, watched (left to right) by Enid Wilson, Lady Heathcoat-Amory (Joyce Wethered), Mme René Lacoste and, with the umbrella, Pam Barton. The first three were his opponents in a novel match at Romford, England, 1938

won the British Ladies' Championship three times running (1931–3) and Pamela Barton became the second woman to hold the British and American titles in the same year since Dorothy Campbell in 1909. She was also, in 1936, the last from abroad to hold the American title until Catherine Lacoste's win in 1969.

In 1935 one of the most remarkable woman athletes ever to have lived gave a series of exhibition matches in the States with Gene Sarazen. In 1932 this athlete, Mildred 'Babe' Didrikson, from Texas, broke the javelin record in the 1932 Olympics. She then broke the record in the high hurdles and came second in the high jump. She could play any sport brilliantly. By 1934 she had decided on golf but though she could easily outdrive the 250-yard marker, her experience was not great enough specially to impress her spec-

tators. They anyhow only wanted to see how powerfully this superstar could perform.

In her later professional career she had great popular success and benefited from Tommy Armour's careful coaching. In 1938 she married George Zaharias, a marriage which settled her and steadied her somewhat wild instincts. But it was not until 1944, when she was reinstated as an amateur, that two of her ambitions could be realized. She became US Ladies' Champion in 1946 and the first American winner of the British Ladies' Championship, in 1947. She then turned professional again and went on to win the US Women's Open Championship in 1948, 1950 and 1954. Tragically she died of cancer in 1956, at the age of forty-one. In 1935 she twice played against Joyce Wethered, when the British player, temporarily deprived of amateur status for working in a sports shop,

Above Enid Wilson, golfer and
journalist, at her beloved
Worplesdon, England. She was
British Ladies' champion 1931-3,
the only player apart from Lady
Margaret Scott (1893-5) to win
this Championship for three
consecutive years
Right A brilliant golfer and
athlete. 'The Babe,' Mildred
Didrikson Zaharias, three times
US Women's Open champion and
winner once of the US and British
amateur titles. She also collected
three gold medals in the 1932
Olympics, for the javelin, 80-metre
hurdles and high jump, though
the latter was confiscated for an
illegal method, the Western roll,
which is now allowed
Far right above 'The Babe,'
Mildred Didrikson Zaharias,
kisses her ball after winning the
US Women's Open at Atlantic
City, NJ, in 1948. She had won
the British Ladies' Championship
in 1947, after which she turned
professional—for the second time

Right The Vicomtesse de Saint Sauveur (Mme Patrick Segard), the great French player. She represented her country from 1937 to 1965 without a break, except, of course, for the war years. She was the British Ladies' champion in 1950 and the French Ladies' Open champion 1948, 1950, 1951 and 1954

toured the United States. The 'Babe' was soundly beaten on both occasions, but one must remember that her golfing skills were then comparatively undeveloped.

As we have seen there were professional women before the Second World War, but it was not until 1946 that the Women's Professional Golfers' Association was formed in the United States by Hope Seignious; its success was short-lived and it was overtaken by a later formation, the Ladies' Professional Golf Association. The first US Women's Open was held in 1946 and won by Patty Berg, the colourful amateur champion of 1938. Today the USGA operates the Women's Open. Among the first and finest women professionals are Betsy Rawls, Louise Suggs, Betty Jameson and above all 'Mickey' Wright.

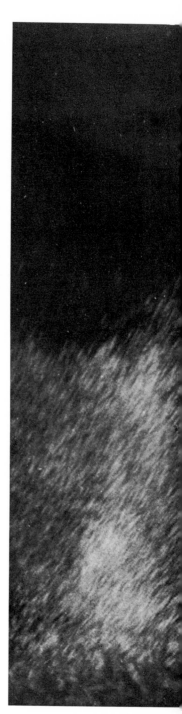

Top left A formidable golfing partnership. Angela and Michael Bonallack, both English Amateur champions and regular internationals. Michael Bonallack has been a member of every British Walker Cup team since 1959 and Angela of the Curtis Cup team from 1956 to 1966
Top right Brigitte Varangot, five times French Ladies' Open champion and a dominant figure for many years in Continental golf
Above Ann Irvin, one of Britain's most consistent women golfers and a Curtis Cup player 1962, 1968 and 1970

Mary Kathryn Wright, who was the US Girls' Amateur Champion in 1952, turned professional in 1954, after being runner-up in the US Ladies' Championship. She went on to capture the US Women's Open Championship in 1958, 1959, 1961 and 1964. Now there are some eighty 'proettes' who compete weekly for ever-growing prize money.

Today France in particular is blessed with many fine players. Catherine Lacoste, the daughter of the British Ladies' 1927 Champion won the US Ladies' Championship in 1969. Brigitte Varangot was the British Ladies' Champion in 1963, 1965 and 1968 and has won the French Ladies' Open Championship five times, and Madame Claudine Cros Rubin is another player, born since 1940, whose skills in the European tournaments are widely appreciated. In Britain, too, a very exciting young player, Michelle Walker, born in 1952, gained her first British Ladies' title in 1971, defended it successfully in 1972 and was runner-up in 1973.

Always a more amateur-biased game than the men's, women's golf is now big business, especially in the United States, but it remains to be seen whether it can ever generate quite the same excitement as its male counterpart.

Catherine Lacoste getting out of a bunker during the 1967 US Women's Open at Hot Springs, Virginia—which she won. In

1969 she was US Ladies' champion, British Ladies' champion, French Ladies' Open champion and French Ladies' Close champion. Forty-two years before, her mother, as Mlle Thion de la Chaume, had also won the British Ladies' Championship

7 The Caddie

AND WHAT OF THE CADDIE? Mary Queen of Scots is the reputed source of the name. She had played the game when she was being schooled in France, where her clubs were borne for her by students – 'les cadets'. The name has grown along with golf, and like golf has become a universally used word. There was the original linksland caddie, more often than not an off-duty fisherman dressed in coarse wool sweater, dark blue to match his seaman's trousers, filling in his time and getting a bit of money between tides. He was a character, taking his client in hand, guiding him and even bullying him, trying to make him win his match. With sand dune, undulating links, and a perspective as unhelpful as a distorting mirror, when even the modern-day pacing of the distance would have been as unhelpful as an intelligent guess, the caddie could tell his employer which club to use.

The caddie is still part of the golf scene, but his end is in sight, as costs rise and the mechanized buggy takes over his purely physical purpose. Only in professional tournaments, where caddies' costs are deductible tax expenses, are they still common, and even then many are but callow youths, with little experience of the course. But there are still the 'regulars', who travel either with their accredited boss or are freelance caddies,

Below Early Victorian golfers and their ragged caddies. Whose 'honour' it was has obviously not been settled
Right Small but respectful caddies, as General Henry Newdigate putts

Left Mrs C. H. Vanderbeck (winner of the US Ladies' Championship in 1915) selects a club from her girl caddie during the French Ladies' Championship at Le Touquet, 1920
Below Again a girl caddie—this time setting a tee for Mrs Bond during the British Ladies' Championship at Burnham, 1923
Top right Henry Cotton congratulates Walter Hagen on winning the British Open Championship for the second year running, while the caddies smile happily—Muirfield, 1929
Below right Barnes, for a time Henry Cotton's permanent caddie, also carried for Leonard Crawley, the English Amateur champion in 1931

'sleeping rough' to reduce their expenses. This is a hard life to live and they must be real lovers of the game to endure it.

The trolley on which the largest bag can be trundled except on the most mountainous courses has made a big difference and it is here to stay. Even the most diehard golfer is becoming inured to the presence of the petrol or electric-driven cart, which has many advantages. Only the fittest can honestly claim not to be tired after four or five miles walking (and searching?) and up to 100 tendon-wrenching swings.

I find that except on a cold or windy day, when the walking exercise helps to warm me up, the golf cart does add enjoyment to golf.

There are many courses, now, where caddies are not available at all and where carts must be used to help speed up play. Students on their long annual holidays can still earn a fair amount of money, carrying clubs and generally helping out, but the day

Top left Practice goes on even after the match
Above This ball picker-upper at the Golf Club of Milan has constructed his own protective equipment
Left Willie Aitchison, Roberto DeVicenzo's caddie, kisses the trophy after DeVicenzo's win in the British Open, Royal Liverpool, 1967
Right Gary Player and 'Rabbit' Dyer, his colourful black caddie, discuss the wind direction on the first tee before the last round of the 1974 British Open at Royal Lytham. In the background Peter Oosterhuis limbers up

of the caddie is slowly disappearing. They are few and far between and are generally spoiled by too affluent regular customers.

Obviously there were early, or comparatively early exceptions, like Francis Ouimet's caddy, the diminutive Edward Lowery, but at the other end of the scale there were the caddies on whom their employers were warned not to spend too much money – in case they dissipated it in drink. In 1900, Horace Hutchinson wrote: 'The professional, as we are now chiefly acquainted with him, is a feckless, reckless, creature.' (Professional *caddie*, of course!)

The good caddie is not simply a beast of burden. He knows the course intimately and can advise his boss on clubs, lies and the state of the greens. I might finish with a famous anecdote which concerned Max Faulkner's faithful 'Mad' Mac. Max, at a loss, asked him how he should hit the ball, to

which the incomparable eccentric replied: 'A wee bit straight, sir.'

8 The Development of Technique

WHENEVER PEOPLE draw me into the subject of how to play golf and get me to talk about styles and methods, I always return to the art of playing the game, and to *The Art of Golf*, published in 1887. Since Sir Walter Simpson wrote this book, golf has come a long way. It may not have been the first book on the Royal and Ancient sport, but it is one of the first that tried to give its readers some idea of the theory of the game. To demonstrate how little new there is in golf (apart from the equipment) I shall quote a few words from the chapter 'On Driving in General':

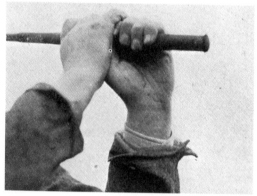

The top pair of photographs show the position of the hands employing the overlapping (Vardon) grip at the start and at the top of the swing. The lower two are of Harry Vardon demonstrating the stance for an intentional slice (left), with the feet behind the ball, and an intentional pull, with the feet in front of the ball
Opposite Aubrey Boomer, five times French Open champion, playing at Dieppe, 1929. By modern standards his stockingette jacket, with its huge pockets for carrying balls, tees and sponges, looks ludicrously unwieldy

Aubrey Boomer
22/6/26

035. J. J. McDERMOTT.—Driving. Top of swing, left side.

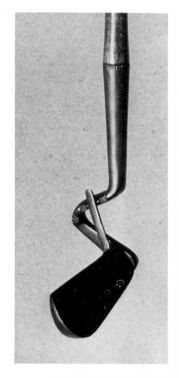

Do I maintain then, the reader may ask, that every one ought to have the same style? By no means. On the contrary, for you or for me to model ourselves on a champion is about as profitless as to copy out *Hamlet* in the hope of becoming Shakespeare. There is no more fruitful source of bad golf than to suppose that there is some best style for each individual, which must be searched out by him, if he is to get the best results out of himself. In a broad and general way, each player ought to have a style which is a reflection of himself, his build, his mind, the age at which he began, and his previous habits.

It is worth pondering that this was written in 1887 and is perhaps one of the most important paragraphs ever assembled on golf and that it is still true today. Yet there are many famous golfers who have produced books in which they single-mindedly pursue one theory and ignore such words of wisdom. I can only believe that they think there is one system only, or alternatively that they are pandering to public demand or to their publisher's edicts. It is worth a passing tribute to Jack Nicklaus that in his book *Golf My Way* he shows his understanding of the game by admitting that he is prepared to adjust his swing in the middle of any round and, if needs be, seek a new gimmick for every day.

In the days of the hickory shaft and the stony gutty (there is no point in tracking back to the days of the feather ball, for then it was essential to nurse the ball to prevent it bursting) players began to play more frequently, since balls had become plentiful and cheap. They would hit the ball as hard as they could and keep by them a bag of practice balls. With the harder hit came the need to insulate the shock of impact – a reason for the thick grips used so generally then. I feel sure that the combination of these thick grips and the leather-faced clubs (the leather helping further to absorb the shock and at the same time protect the beechwood heads) made the grip on the club work for the palms, rather than for the fingers as today. Whilst those teachers of old did not ignore the grip,

Left and right The advance of photographic technique. John McDermott, the first home-bred American to win the US Open Championship (1911) is caught at the top of his swing by a stereoscopic camera. The very famous multiple photograph of Bob Jones's driving swing consists of 61 exposures of 1/100,000 sec. spaced at 1/100 sec. intervals

Below One of the first adjustable irons, with a simple ratchet to enable the head to be set at various lofts. Inevitably ill-balanced, such clubs have also always been rejected by the Royal and Ancient

one has only to examine photographs of golfers playing some eighty years ago to realize that the shaft was free to slide about in the hands. It amazes me that with such loose grips Harold Hilton, John Ball Jr, H. G. Hutchinson, J. L. Low and Edward Blackwell, among many top amateurs at the end of the last century, could win fame – and matches. For these great names would hold their clubs in the palms of both hands, left thumbs outside the grip, letting their hands slide up and down during the swing, a 'fault' we would strongly condemn today. But then in the same era there were J. H. Taylor, Harry Vardon, James Braid, L. Balfour-Melville, R. Maxwell and John Graham, who gripped their clubs in a manner which we would find perfectly acceptable. The modern overlapping grip is, of course, accredited to Harry Vardon, though there is evidence that Leslie Balfour-Melville used it first and that J. H. Taylor, using this very grip, was winning before

Vardon scored his first major successes. Perhaps it is just that Harry Vardon was so frequently photographed that the grip became associated with him.

'Keep your eye on the ball' is by no means a new slogan. It has been an essential maxim in golf since the game started, and the fact that you could stare at the ball *too* much has not escaped notice either.

Another tip for players, offered at least as early as the 1880s, before the overlapping grip was recognized as an aid to promoting co-operation between the hands, was that they should keep their hands as near together as possible. Sir Walter Simpson went as far as warning players that for every inch the hands were apart, ten yards would be forfeited on the shot. I have never personally equated the adoption of such grips with inches and yards, but I imagine that Sir Walter must have calculated his figures from his own experiences.

199

Today style, as such, seems to be given a smaller and smaller place in the game and no one really cares too much if some players actually look elegant when they play – only results talk.

Fortunately it does still happen that most of the great players today look absolutely grand when they make their strokes; but there are winners who appear quite unorthodox and employ styles which confound many an accepted theory. Years ago style was admired, almost worshipped I suppose – and this went for life in general as well. Now, sheer beauty has been overtaken by utility and efficiency. Then, style was seen as an essential part of the make-up of every golfer; today, unless it justifies the end, it is almost ignored. With the notable exception of J. H. Taylor (who was a short, sturdy player, exceptionally strong for his size), all the great golfers of yesteryear had long free swings and seemed to throw themselves about much more as they hit. The ball itself almost certainly had much to do with this, for unless you have swung at a gutty you cannot imagine how unresponsive it was and how much effort went into driving it 200 yards. As a young man I often used the gutty in exhibition matches against the seniors, who would be playing with the more conventional ball of the time.

The surprising fact which emerges when getting down to a comparative study of styles and methods of yesterday and today is that they are fundamentally so nearly similar that the hints of yesterday can apply today and tomorrow.

Here is a series of 'dos' and 'don'ts' of those days. They were written over eighty years ago by Sir Walter Simpson, and my own comments follow them. They remain as enlightening to today's readers as they did, no doubt, to the readers in knickerbockers, cap and Norfolk jacket:

Don't take the club back too quickly. This advice can surely never change, for otherwise it puts a lot of extra strain on the hands.

James Braid plays from loose sand, 1922. Note that his head is kept well down, with the right hand forcing the club head past the left. After the ball has left the club face he still retains perfect balance

Don't hurry the downward swing, but allow the club naturally to increase speed. This is the old way of saying 'swing the club head', a slogan that brings in countless dollars to instructors in the USA and elsewhere.

Don't think of the circle described in the swing as being vertically up and down the line of flight of the ball as in cricket. Golfers in the early days claimed most of their successful adherents from the cricket field, but already in those days the path of the clubhead was not seen as a circle but as a looping movement. This shows that all the astonishment expressed by the golfing world on discovering that Bob Jones's swing was looping as it was flowing displayed ignorance, for it was well known, years earlier, that a golf clubhead does not follow a perfect circular route.

Don't swing any club so far back as to lose control of it. Today we might say 'don't overswing' or, as I wrote in my first golf book when talking of the three-quarter swing, that it is preferable to hold on to the club all the time and be restricted by the flexibility of the left wrist to a less than full swing, if getting the swing to the horizontal means letting go of the club in the hands.

Don't forget the clubhead should be travelling at its greatest velocity when it reaches the ball, having gradually increased in speed with no perceptible pause from the top of the swing. Today this would be described as 'a late hit', but the 'no perceptible pause from the top of the swing' seems hard to explain, unless to keep the swing smooth throughout.

Don't hit at the ball. The rhythm of the swing must not be destroyed. Slow back means that time must be given to allow the clubhead to gain speed gradually until the highest momentum is reached just prior to the point of impact. This is, to some extent, a repetition of previous advice, but 'wait for the hit' might apply. The softer, more whippy hickory shaft needed a different timing from our modern steel shaft. (Now, after forty years of steel shafts, there has

arrived a light carbon-fibre shaft with torsion which has the timing and a feel of the hickory shaft. Has this come to stay? As I write I do not know, but, as I hope I have shown, this new shaft has completed the cycle. Where do we go from here?)

Don't in swinging back take the clubhead so far out that the right elbow has to leave the side. This again is advice against swinging too upright.

Don't bend the left knee too soon with wood clubs in the upward swing. 'Keep the left heel down as long as possible in the back swing' might be more in line with today's parlance.

Don't swing so much with iron clubs, but take them back rather more upright than in driving. Here the word 'upright' appears, which is self-explanatory; but a simpler expression would be 'use a shorter swing with iron clubs'. Iron clubs can be swung on the same arc, more or less, as the woods. The swing need only be more upright because the ball is nearer to the player.

Don't wrist mashie shots. Allow the arms and hands to work as one. Here is a distinction between the flick and the push; the wrist mashie shot is the flick; the push would be the forerunner of what is today's stiff-wristed wedge shot. How true it is that most shots, except possibly the little delicate chips, are forearm and wrist, not wrist alone, unless expressly played this way.

Do let the wrist take the clubhead back first, let the arms follow, then let the body turn from the hips. In the downswing, the body turns immediately, and the body turns again and finally faces the hole on the finish. Today we say: 'Let the arms and hands take back the club together, let the body follow, begin to unwind the body and let the club follow.' The body unwinds, checks an instant only for the clubhead to pass the body, then continues after impact.

Do keep the head steady throughout the swing. There should be no jumping up either at the top of the swing or at the moment of impact. 'Play under the head' would be a simple way of telling the golfer not to permit himself to move his head all over the place.

Don't look up too soon after the ball is struck. Cricketers are apt to do this. Why only cricketers, one might ask? For it is a general universal complaint for which there is no certain trick cure. The only way to overcome this fault is simply not to do it – to have educated hands, in other words.

Do look at the part of the ball to be struck, not at the ball in an absent-minded, abstract kind of way. Focus on the back of the ball, not just on the ball in general. 'Concentrate on where you are to make impact' is the modern advice.

It might seem that by making these comparisons I am trying to make out there is nothing new under the sun. The comparisons amount to very little, for the advice offered over eighty years ago stands today. My own opinion is that as the game has grown and more people have studied it, one can put the study (and the players of the day have inspired such study) into periods. The balls and implements, as much as the players, have been responsible for the trends; the improvement in courses has also had an effect on technique during these periods. It is correct to say that with the hickory shaft a larger variety of strokes could be played – intentionally and unintentionally. Now the almost torsionless steel shaft of recent times has simplified stroke production. The average dud and duffer may refute the suggestion that his counterpart of pre-steel-shaft days could play the ball in a greater variety of ways than he can. But it *was* true, for he would have had the torsion in the hickory shaft to contend with and help him. The combination of hickory shaft and golf balls of various weights and sizes (a state of affairs which endured until 1 May 1921 when the standard 1.62in./1.62oz ball was first made to The Royal and Ancient specifications) made a great variety of trajectories the rule rather

Left Henry Cotton driving at the 3rd during the first round of the 1934 British Open Championship. The body is balanced, the right side is well through, and the right heel has fully left the ground now that the stroke is finished, creating balance and smoothness
Right Bunkered and slightly anxious, Henry Cotton has followed on with the club head after the ball, the guarantee of a successful shot

than the exception.

Players, as now, moulded their styles to suit their strength but would also include in their calculations the type of ball being used. The small, heavy ball suited certain methods, but was difficult to get in the air, so apart from requiring great strength to send it on its way, it was usually cut up 'through the green' to get it airborne.

The time from the first rubber-cored ball, the Haskell, in 1902 to the adoption, by the Royal and Ancient, of the standard ball (still unchanged today in the British zone) in 1921 could count as one period. 1921–9 (when the steel shaft came in) could be another period, and 1929 to the present day a third period. During this third period American influence in style and method became more pronounced. The breakaway in 1929 from the 'British' ball, on the grounds that it made golf too easy (yet was difficult to play from the thicker, watered, clovery fairways), and the adoption in 1932 of the 1.68in./1.62oz ball (still used today in

the United States, as it now is in professional golf tournaments and in the Open championships in Britain and on the Continent) meant a slightly different technique to keep the naturally higher flying ball under the same control. The latest news is that the makers have now produced the large size ball with a lower trajectory, like a small ball in fact. It is surprising it has taken so long to arrive, for this is a wonderful ball and the method of 'pushing' it to keep it down will not be needed.

In the 1920s Bob Jones, Walter Hagen and Gene Sarazen, brought up on hickory and the small ball, reigned supreme in the world of golf and their reign just spilled over into the 1930s. Before them, the methods of Braid, Vardon and Taylor, our heroes and the pattern of the day, have withstood the test of time, and I might humbly add myself to this list as a further example of a golfer using his wrists to the best advantage and playing 'open to shut'. These great players were able to keep up a reasonable standard of play for long

years and also devote time to other things in life, whereas it seems to me that since the end of World War II the top golfers have needed to hit off hundreds of balls, and nearly every day, simply to make their play sound enough. Walter Hagen said to me on one occasion (we had many games together) that if he had had to slog at the game like present-day golfers in order to reach and keep his form he would have chosen another profession. Possibly the perfect woman golfer, Joyce Wethered, was another example of a wrist-under-the-shaft golfer, getting into form with minimum effort – one might say a natural golfer. And today Gary Player, Arnold Palmer and Johnny Miller all favour the 'open to shut' method, which Sam Snead has used so well and for such a long time. There is no strain on the back of the hands and the arms are in charge.

These success cases I have just cited could be attributable to inborn ability, but I cannot help but feel that method has something to do with it – especially in Gary Player's recent play. The very strong hitters – and there are many in post-war golf – will always be able to flight the ball better than the weaker players, which means preventing the ball climbing too high and sacrificing itself to the mercy of the wind. This is one reason why there was a move for at least two decades towards a more closed club face at the top of the backswing. There is a limit to how straight faced a driver can be, and to the depth of the face, as many youngsters have found out. Many young golfers will have experimented with 'putter-straightfaced' drivers to see if they can make the ball go further, but this has been proved a waste of time, and even big hitters, like Arnold Palmer, need to have at least ten degrees loft on the face of their drivers, for a golf ball can be gripped on a lofted club face, where the loft is diminished as the ball is struck, better than on a straight faced club where the ball is hit upwards. The spin is essential to control the flight.

The Gutty-ball Period

There is not much left in golf today, apart from old clubs in clubhouse and museum showcases, to remind us of the game as it was in the gutty-ball era, when it was really beginning to develop. Although the gutty was introduced in 1848, the game grew but slowly and by 1896 there were only 61 courses in Scotland, 46 in England and some 80 in the USA. Wooden-headed clubs for approach shots were gradually ousted by long-headed iron ones, but now, funnily enough, we have returned to wooden headed clubs, for I have seen wooden golf clubs number 1–7, and I don't understand how it is possible to grade golf clubs with wooden heads to produce such a loft. All the same there exists an entire set of wooden clubs, which is turning the clock back 150 years with a vengeance, but they only sell in limited numbers, usually to golfers who dread a 'shank' and are as weak as kittens!

J. H. Taylor was the first English-born player to show the Scots that golfing well was not solely their prerogative; he launched the mashie, a short-faced lofted iron for pitching. This would have been, I suppose, today's no. 7 iron. Golfers began to score better as the gutty ball improved in composition and markings, and probably also because the balls stood up better to the practising required to perfect a good swing. The unresilient gutty was a hard ball to propel and it needed a terrific sweeping stroke to send it on its way – the more sweep the better, for the shock of impact then seemed less. Admittedly its stony lifelessness made play round the green simpler, for the ball never 'got away' from the player and made a fabulous impact noise – a wonderful ball to putt with.

Scores in the old days were ridiculously high by our standards, and any attempt to make comparisons with the period almost 100 years later must be unwise, for a golfer whose lifespan took him from the days of young Tom Morris's Championship Belt win at Prestwick in 1870 to recent times (the course was only 12 holes) said that his score of 149 for 36 holes (three times round) was but 2 over par, as par, by our standards, was 49 for the 12 holes.

No doubt there were stylists before Harry Vardon, but he, because his swing seemed to give as good as or better results than any contemporary, with less apparent effort, was known as 'The Stylist'. Controlled shots have obviously always been played, for shots of this type only came to be considered obsolete when batteries of iron clubs appeared, even numbered in half numbers ($2\frac{1}{2}$, $3\frac{1}{2}$, etc), with whose help it was assumed that one swing was good enough for the whole game. The popular wooden putter seemed to die with the gutty, though there are a few fans still loyal to it. This long-headed club, one of the original and most used amongst the few carried loosely under the arm, was employed for any sort of approach shot, at times from as far back as 100 yards from the hole, particularly on such hard-baked, bare fairways as were likely to be found at certain

Joyce Wethered practises with the left hand at Ashridge (1938), where Henry Cotton was professional. Perfect position, perfect balance and the shot travelled nearly 90 yards with a no. 6 iron

Leopoldo Ruiz, a fine Argentinian golfer, about to use his right hand to the full. Players have to get the club head to arrive at the ball with the left hand and shaft in line at impact

periods of the year on links like St Andrews. The few older golfers prized these handmade treasures of bygone days, but as no top-grade golfer had used one for years it can be concluded that for modern golf they really are obsolete.

Rubber-cored Ball Days
It is obviously just a coincidence that with the advent of the Haskell, the first satisfactory rubber-cored ball, when golf took a big leap forward in popularity, the camera became a sufficiently improved apparatus to freeze the swings of the leading players and so open up the study of what took place during a golf swing. Some years later, the slow-motion cinecamera decisively exploded a number of theories, in particular the one that the perfect swing was a true circular movement, whereas in fact it is a looping swing. Sir Walter Simpson had already said this in 1887, as I have mentioned. The rubber-cored ball managed to turn the ordinary clumsy golfer overnight into a moderate performer – for even mis-hits gave a 75 per cent result. The long hitters were obliged to learn control, and so arose the controlled backswings for play to the pin, and the use of the more lofted clubs which imparted greater backspin and therefore more ball control.

From 1902 to 1921 players had every opportunity to get the most out of themselves, for there was no limit to the size and weight of ball they could use, and of course extremes were tested. Small, heavy balls and small and large 'floaters' all appeared and appealed to various people, but naturally they complicated the game. In a single round the golfer was inclined to use a small and heavy ball against the wind and a larger ball downwind, hoping to achieve the maximum out of himself. Or if he did not do so, regretting that he had not tried the 'other ball'!

Despite these conditions, and the fact that artificial watering to keep the greens holding was not encouraged, the Open Championship in Britain was held as usual in mid-summer. By then the putting greens were often shiny, brown, skating rinks, which forced the player to learn to play all the shots to the green and there is no doubt that in this never ending search to beat the game the hickory shaft was a help. With the torsion in the hickory shaft and the fine adjustment to the feel of any club which filing or scraping the wood could achieve, golfers could carry out experiments which are impossible today, as there are only a half-dozen grades of steel shaft to choose from. However, the new carbon-graphite shaft, which at the time of writing is still in its trial stages, has offered as many as seventeen different whips (now being reduced for commercial reasons) which could, naturally, appeal to the real student of the game. I imagine that these new shafts too can be scraped or filed down to give any personal feel required, but their cost is so high that few golfers would risk altering the feel at the hazard of ruining an expensive piece of equipment. But again it means that the wheel has come a full revolution back almost to where golf, as we know it, was born.

In this 1902–21 period it seems that the golfer to be successful had to be a smart person, for he had to work out the exact shot he wanted and he had a big variety of strokes in his repertoire from which to choose. The hands, always most important for the part they play in the swing, became even more important. A peep at George Beldam's excellent book *Great Golfers, their Methods at a Glance*, published in 1904, will show how golfers of that day had time, with a flexible torsionful hickory shaft, to make the shots with their hands. The pitch and run shot was played with a most pronounced turnover of the wrists, forearms and shoulders, and a cut-up pitch was played with a definite slicing action across the ball, left elbow riding high, cutting off the 'legs' of the ball, as it were.

These exaggerated actions almost seem to be caricatures today, and appear as dated as the acting in the first silent films. Yet little has changed fundamentally in these methods. For a golf ball, of necessity, since it conforms to the strict laws of ballistics, responds to the same spins, and Arnold Palmer seems to me to be the one golfer playing the game in the most natural possible way, for many of his finishes at the end of his strokes give away the type of shot he has set out to play.

Players in this era began to practise more, because competition was fiercer and it became ever more necessary to specialize. Yet prior to the First World War, players in both professional and amateur ranks would often not begin to polish up their game until a week before the championships.

Braid, Vardon and Taylor dominated golf in this period. They had varying styles because they were of distinctly different builds. Braid, tall and wiry, and when at his best very flexible, was 6ft 1½in. tall and weighed 174lbs (12st 6lbs); Vardon, 5ft 9½in. and 154lbs (11st), was very wiry and supple; Taylor, 5ft 8½in. and 161lbs (11st 7lbs), was short and sturdy. They all played with their left wrists under the top of the shaft at the top of the swing, and this became the position to copy. It was not that other players did not keep the left wrist in line with the forearm, now spoken of as the latest 'square to square' method, but I am sure that the different equipment then used, and also the weight and type of ball used, had a greatly varying influence on the methods of individual players. Balls would fly with every sort of trajectory, for the makers knew little then of the effect various flight markings on the covers of the balls would have. Even in my lifetime, and Gene Sarazen confirms this, we have had to search through a box of balls to find good ones to use in serious play. Now testing equipment has made this unnecessary.

John Ball Jr, who had an exceptional record as an amateur, using gutties in the last years of the century, employed the so-called latest American method, 'square to square', as long ago as that – though he did have a curious double-handed power grip, with the right hand so far under that the fingers of that hand faced the sky. I use this name ironically when referring to this method, for I find many

Doug Ford (USPGA champion 1955, winner of US Masters 1957) was one of the great putters of his day, and the first of the tap putters. Here the club head has stopped and the ball is already well clear of the club face

young Americans today breaking their backs practising, believing that it is the secret of golf – and quite new. I am certain that players of the calibre of Braid, Vardon and Taylor (the order in which I put these great names is of no importance) had all the shots, and used them to exercise their superiority over their contemporaries. I am sure that they had all tried out this shut-face method – Braid, in fact, owing to his left hand being more on top of the shaft than was the case with the other two, was at times a big hooker as a result of this tendency.

The shut-to-open-face player can, of course, play very straight shots – the records of those using this method prove it – but the records also show that very few of them escape periods, long periods at that, when a disastrous hook has put them off their game. Many never recover their youthful form, for shut-face golf is a young man's golf, and they pursue the same method in the hope of recapturing that 'something' which once gave them their greatest golfing days. The shut-face player fights a hook, and the open-face player generally has a slice as his nightmare. To be a good golfer anyway it is necessary to have one side of the course to play towards. By that I mean that every player has a safe side, a side on which he knows the ball is not likely to go when he is under the greatest pressure.

Although the rubber-cored ball was a good product, it needed flighting all the time to get the best out of it, just as would a 'floater', if used today. In those days, with a wind from the left, it would be necessary to fade the ball in order to steal a few yards, and likewise to hook with the wind when it came from the right. The modern powerful tournament player can ignore almost any wind except a gale. Today many players repeat one swing monotonously, finding that it is plenty good enough for the vast majority of occasions.

Although the three heroes of The Triumvirate were by no means weak men, sheer power in golf, as such, was not worshipped then as it was to become later. Skill reaped its reward – skill at conceiving the shots; skill at executing them; skill at judging distance. Nobody measured the distances they had to play – a pity, perhaps, for then we should all have scored better. When the gutty was *the* ball, a strong but whippy shaft was prized, but it was found that for control under pressure a somewhat firmer shaft was preferable, and hence the straight-grained 'steely' hickory shaft came to be in demand. This demand grew as the game developed in popularity. Hickory wood was used in the construction of motor-car wheel spokes and tool handles too and grew scarce, so good hickory shafts became more and more difficult to find.

When the war ended in 1918, players were using very mixed bags of clubs. It was one of the joys of golf to search the racks of the professional's shop at each course visited to find a new super club to fit into one's set. Then the next task was to learn to know that club, to adjust one's game to the club and to remember when playing it how it had to be timed, if the shot could be forced or not. Some shafts would not take an all-out hit; they had to be timed, and this timing learned. With a big bag of clubs it was more than likely that every club would behave differently, owing to its different weight and balance. Even a good iron club would soon be rubbed away with emery cloth by conscientious caddies, and so soft iron heads got lighter every day as they were cleaned to remove the rust. Then came the stainless-steel head, a logical development. Golfers, indeed, had many more problems than today, but it was great fun, looking for ideal clubs; odd clubs and, with iron clubs, seeking to keep them from getting too dry, for the heads would become loose, if stored in a hot place, even overnight. What a panic, too, to push them into a bucket of water to make them tight enough for the round.

Period 1921–9

I take these years following World War I as another definite period in golf, because in 1921 a standard golf ball of not less than 1.62in. in diameter and not more than 1.62oz in weight came into being. (The correspondence of the two figures is coincidental.) This disposed, at a stroke of the complications of having to choose your ball for the day and the course, according to local conditions, and meant that golfers at least had one problem solved for them. There were some faint objections, of course, but it was a sound move, for players could now set about learning to master one ball, the same for everyone. (It is thought that in the next decade all championship players may be using one 'anonymous' ball to avoid each maker providing specials.) From this moment mechanical golf, as we were later to see and read about, was created. For all over the world golfers began to practise hard to learn about this new standard ball. Methods of play stopped differing widely from each other, although Bob Jones of Atlanta, Georgia, the top golfer in the game at this time (and apart from Walter Hagen well out on his own) set the whole world trying to play golf with a narrow stance, at times so narrow that his heels were practically touching, even for full shots. Only Walter Hagen's wide, sprawly stance reminded golfers that there could be champions with other positions. 'Bobby' Jones (as he will ever be called by British golfers, although he curiously enough disliked being called Bobby and always signed his letters Bob) turned professional after his 'Grand Slam' wins of 1930 – the British Open and Amateur and the American Open and Amateur Championships. This period of narrow stance experiments (I myself used the narrow stance with mixed success like many others at the time) came to an end in due course, and I think that, like the Naughty Nineties, the Fabulous Twenties, will never return. Jones's long lazy swing was photographed in slow motion, watched on cardboard photo flickers, and analysed by writers and students round the world. It had its effect on the world's golf game for a number of years.

Few golfers hit past the chin and under the head better than Ben Hogan. He had the firmest grip of the club of them all, and the shaft just vibrated as he made contact with the ball

spend his quota of practice time – in the vast majority of cases without profit – in testing out the new-found freedom of the wrists he felt when swinging clubs with this interlocking grip, left thumb outside. (With the left thumb inside the palm of the right hand fingers interlocked there is a tendency to push the ball, in my own game, so I use overlapping – and besides it hurts the little finger of my right hand a lot.)

Many golfers have used this Morrison type of grip successfully. The Whitcombes, Sarazen, Ouimet and Nicklaus come to mind right away; but it was not the grip for everyone, and like a Wall Street boom its wayward popularity did not last, and even with the great influence of Nicklaus, perhaps the best player ever to date, it has not gained in popularity against the now almost universal overlapping grip.

Since scores and records began to be noted, it has been obvious, in Willy Park's oft quoted remark, that 'a man who could putt was a match for anyone'. But although, for example, the French professional Arnaud Massy and Jack White, two early British Open champions, were celebrated for their putting, it was not until the 1921–9 period that the good putters began to be very much noticed. Players who, on the gradually improving putting surfaces, could regularly rely on getting by with brilliant putting (when the rest of their game was below first-class average) became more numerous, and golfers with inferior long games began to win events through skilful performances on and around the greens. How could this happen all of a sudden? I believe it was because competition and analysis showed more clearly the supreme value of good putting, and the model round with 36 putts, two per green, was soon out of date. It had to be 33 putts at the most, and today 30, 29, 28 and even 26 is the standard aimed at, and in fact required, to win.

In addition, the post-war conditions found courses easier than before. Less rough had been kept because of the golf-ball scarcity and the high cost of the ball. History is now

Overlapping, yet not overlapping but interlocking the latter part of this Jones period and the next few years into the 1930s, came a bestselling book by Alex Morrison from California, in which the interlocking grip – index finger of the right hand intertwined with the little finger of the left and the left thumb outside the grip – was put forward as the 'latest' in golf. Vardon had said of his own grip in 1904, 'my grip is overlapping not interlocking', so clearly he had tried this grip which clutched the golf world, and it took quite a long time for each and every golfer to repeating itself some fifty years later, with one great difference: courses are already easier to start with. When courses are easy, whether they be long or short matters little, and with insufficient rough to punish erring shots, everything hinges on the putting. You cannot win on a superlative long game as you could at one time on a punishing course. Players today are inclined to grumble about bad rough on a course, complaining that it ruins their scores. What will the public think if their average is ruined? This may sound pathetic, but some professional players will actually not play in a tournament on a tough course for fear that their average will be spoilt. The chances of a lost ball in the wilderness became less with the construction of courses on open land, for with the fast growth of the game and courses springing up everywhere it was not always possible to find ground with natural features, and also, since playing 18 holes was taking a progressively longer time, time wasted in searching for balls was 'not on' economically, fewer rounds were played per day on ever lengthening courses.

The day of the recovery player, down in two from everywhere, had arrived. Walter Hagen, the first of a great line of golfers who did not rely entirely on mechanical stroke production, like, for example, Vardon and Taylor, to win, became a master of rolling three shots into two when greens were missed with erring shots. He had no 'sand iron' to help him. He had to use, as did other players of that era, such as Ted Ray and James Braid, who had reputations for making fabulous recoveries, ordinary niblicks with thin soles. Hagen, while including explosion shots in his repertoire, had much faith in his ability to flick the ball cleanly off the sand, a dangerous shot in very little use today. It is often said that the big flanged sole on the wedge and sand iron has ruined the game because it makes bunker play too easy and takes away the fear of being bunkered and that the width of the sole should be controlled. Even from a very teed-up ball in sand, the modern professional will blast the ball on to the green with

Martin Roesink, from Holland, is one of the longest hitters in the game. Here, at the finish of a drive, though his body has pivoted to face down the fairway, the left foot is still firmly clamped to the ground. The hands are high and the follow through is as full as they come

his skid-soled sand club. This is in fact a much safer shot, made possible for him by the broad skid sole of the modern sand iron.

I feel that golf owes one particular debt of gratitude amongst many to James Braid for the way in which he kept the courses at the British club Walton Heath, in Surrey – such fine tests of golf. They are still great tests, though watering, often excessive alas, has spoilt their character to a great extent today. At courses like the Walton Heath one's bad shots are always punished by the narrowness of the heather-lined fairways, a state of affairs which seems to be disappearing today, for golf is developing into a game of strength and most holes are too wide open and big hitters can carry bunkers placed to trap the average players.

It was during this period, the mid-twenties,

that the matched set of clubs, numbered instead of named, first appeared, a further step towards mechanical golf. The theory advanced was that you bought your set, used one swing only, got a good caddie to give you the right club, and hey presto! you were off. The matched set, numbered one to nine, originated in America, and so did the ballyhoo that went with it. It spread fast and soon golfers everywhere were wanting to learn the swing that matched the clubs. This swing, under Bob Jones's influence at that time, was a long one, a real swing at the ball again.

In 1928, at the age of twenty-one, I went to the States to see why they were beating our home players so regularly and found that steel shafts were already legal and one type of bigger ball was in use, and I actually played my first tournaments in America with hickory shafts. About this time, Horton Smith, aged twenty, a tall skinny young man from Joplin, Missouri, was cleaning up on the Winter Circuit. He had not known anything but golf with steel shafts and had knocked all the fancy shot-making frills off by just simply scoring low, using the same swing and same shot for practically all his strokes – a gently hooking ball which was to be the dread of the experienced golfers he was later to succeed. He used a slow, deliberate three-quarter swing, which he repeated mechanically for every shot. He somehow never took three putts and he holed a lot of good ones under the greatest pressure; he became renowned as a super putter.

This was rather like the way Bobby Locke played in the 1950s, though Locke's swing was longer and faster. Seeing Horton Smith play was quite a revelation, for I saw straight-away that the day of learning to play all the shots was almost over – the steel shafts had made golf an easier game. Only one swing was necessary, and I had to find out as soon as possible the swing which would suit me. The soft, watered greens, a necessity in a country where the fixed fine weather periods of spring, summer and autumn meant many successive sunny days and no rain, showed that one shot, if you could repeat it, was good enough to win any event, if you could putt. This fact did not really register in Britain until the steel shaft was legalized. At last everyone could have the exact set used by his favourite champion, a set which would not vary with the weather, as was always the case with hickory shafts when iron heads got loose if kept in too dry a place overnight, as I have said.

The Steel Shaft Days – 1930 Onwards
Gradually the top golfers began to realize that golf was a more simple game with this new standard link between the hands and the clubhead. It was not necessary to know or to practise all the shots as in the hickory-shaft days in order to know your clubs individually, though some of the older players never quite adapted themselves to steel. Abe Mitchell, whose play I have always admired and who was a great golfer and wonderful striker himself of the ball, never got to like steel. He could not make himself play just one stroke; he liked among other things to fade many shots up to the flag and found the steel shaft could let him down when he attempted to play a controlled fade, or any special stroke for that matter. I guess he missed the torsion of the hickory shaft. His contemporary, George Duncan, was also too much of an artist to enjoy steel. They would both have rejoiced at the coming of the carbon-fibre shafts.

As the leading players of the day were of course all brought up on the hickory shaft, it was only natural that there should be a search, for a time, to produce a steel shaft with the qualities of hickory. This led to a series of shafts being produced with torsion. Usually they had some sort of split or even a dent in the shaft, but these experiments proved to be a failure. The torsion effect was too fast to control. Then it was realized that the steel shaft with no torsion was nearer to the ideal one for all. Whip it could have, but the less torsion the better. There had been various sorts of shafts, from the limber type built to feel like a fishing rod at one end of the range, to pokers at the other end, and of course average whips in between. The 'Dynamic' range, a name given to an early shaft with steps in it, was very popular and an excellent shaft. It is making a comeback as I write these words. It has now been reborn, after being superseded since 1935 by many other (better?) types. But it has certainly been the most nearly torsionless steel shaft, with varying degrees of whip, which has contributed no doubt to lower and lower scoring.

As golf became an industry, and a big one at that, exploiters of golf courses realized that in order to make the turnstiles click healthily, the number of players using a course per day had to be increased. So the rough began to disappear faster than ever to enable quicker rounds to be played and to give the customers a greater feeling of enjoyment.

Then came World War II and again a shortage of golf balls, making a lost ball nearly a tragedy; and when the war ended in 1945 so many golfers had got used to playing round the 'park' that days of rough as we used to know them had ended. This open-field trend has had such an effect on golf, together with the arrival of television, that long driving has come to be worshipped. All the top players throughout the world hit the ball full out all the time and do not pay much penalty for errors of direction – nor do they expect to do so, except in the major Open championships, where the courses are specially prepared to create as tough a test as possible. I find very open park courses tedious and boring to play. I do not only mean that I find them easier to play than good courses, or that I score low on them, but they do not inspire me and I feel all the time that my good shots are not rewarded sufficiently. I seem to score the same on the good as on the bad layouts.

Betting, now a big part of golf, has developed I'm sure to provide interest while playing on monotonous courses. In one recent US championship I read that players and the press, who were backing them, were objecting to three-inch-long rough round and behind the putting surfaces, because the lies were poor and accurate chipping impossible. This particular rough might have been extra lush, but rough should always exist somewhere on a golf course; it is part of the game.

Courses are longer today but in the main easier. The extra yardage added does not seem to compensate for a lack of natural difficulties and now there is a definite leaning towards the use of forward tees for some early rounds in big competitions in order to encourage low scoring for publicity purposes and to bring in the crowds.

Since 1941 there has been a general trend to use and recommend a more shut club face *at the top of the swing*, and this fashion has been in vogue ever since, until almost five years ago, when I did notice that less was talked of the back of the left hand facing the sky. Since then players have moved their left hands back on the shaft to show two knuckles, which is what I have always recommended and used. The value of this change is to make more use of the hands and to cut out some of the body unwind, which had a tendency to be exaggerated and put more strain on the spine, which was more than the human frame could stand, sometimes causing serious permanent damage. No game is worth playing if it brings such tragedies.

Somehow in the last ten years there has been a tendency to write about golf as being a game where 50 per cent of the action is body and 50 per cent is arms and hands. I have never seen a golf ball hit with this proportion of power. I still feel that golf is a game of 85 per cent hand and arms and 15 per cent body. Practising with the steel shaft was easier, because full pressure could be applied all the time without spoiling the shaft, and given enough energy and practice an unusual swing could be made to give results, at least while the confidence held. The larger ball, which naturally tended to fly higher, needed to be knocked down to get a lower ball in flight with the maximum control, and so this led to strong players closing the club face

Above Sam Torrance, a promising young Scottish professional, building up his strength by striking at an old tire. This very successful general exercise can be done with the hands separately
Right Arnold Palmer plays a tee shot during the 1965 Piccadilly World Match-Play Tournament. His head has stayed well down and he has allowed the club head to do the work. The right leg, with the heel just leaving the ground, is thrusting against the left side

prior to impact much more than golfers had been doing previously; but with the new lower-trajectory big ball the 'old-fashioned' method is back again.

One long driver of modern times who really kept his wrist under the shaft like Harry Vardon has been Jimmy Thompson, the North Berwick boy who went to the States. Because of this style he hit a very high-flying ball. Now big-hitting Jim Dent, a black pro, who Nicklaus admits hits up to 60 yards past him off the tee, plays 'open to shut' with 'lots of wrist action' – his quote.

Up to 1929 I always had a practice set and a tournament set of clubs, saving the latter so as not to wear them out, but since those days one favourite set has been enough. And since then, of course, the restriction on the number of clubs permitted to a player in competition golf was obvious legislation, for as shaft breakages are almost unheard of today it is

quite silly to carry over twenty clubs round a golf course as lots of players did prior to 1929. Fourteen clubs became the limit. This in fact had no effect on the scoring, or for that matter on club sales. The tendency with steel shafts has been for divots to get bigger and bigger, for no strain was too much for the shaft. If the wrists could stand it the shafts could.

Players like powerful Sam Snead (one of the game's great players and, now over sixty, able to hold his place in the best company) were taking platefuls of earth in order to get the maximum grip on the ball, for the USGA ruling that face markings were to be almost decorative caused the players to hit the ball steeper in order to grip it well on the club face. This ruling, since confirmed in Britain, came out because for a short time there was a sort of competition as to how rough a club face could be made, and a cold chisel and hammer were used to deepen the face grooves on standard club markings or a punch to widen and deepen the dots used as face markings. The very slotted club faces, apart from ruining a golf ball at almost every stroke, caused the ball to fly lower, and so there came into being a low-flying pitch to the pin, which had much backspin on it, caused by these face markings. It was christened a 'wedge-shot'. The club generally used was the wedge, a broad-soled niblick with a wide flange bottom to the head. The back edge of the sole of this club did not ride high as in the 'Sand-wedge', 'Dynamiter', 'Howitzer' or special sand clubs with such trade names, which were made to skid through the sand and so do away with the risk of digging into the sand and fluffing the ball.

The sand-wedge, which came out in the 1930s, was a sensation at the time. The first models were egg-shaped, hollow-faced clubs with a high back edge on the sole, so that the club skidded and did not dig into the sand or earth. The hollow face, soon to be ruled illegal, because it hit the ball twice, it was alleged, as the ball ran up the club face on being squeezed, was the club which everybody had to have, and of course today, with its normal flat face and skid sole, is to be found in the bag of every golfer. Sand-wedges have improved since the early days and now there is one popular type, which I have already mentioned, which has a high back edge which readily skids through on hitting sand or turf. This club is used mainly for bunker work, but a wedge, known as a 'pitching wedge' is also in most sets. The extra weight of its thick sole is considered valuable for recovery shots and pitching to a green, though the vast majority of golfers would do better forgetting it, and using a no. 7, no. 8 or no. 9 instead.

The longer I live the more things, as I have said, seem to go in cycles. For example, in 1848 the solid gutty ball came in and it reigned supreme until the rubber-cored ball with the thin cover took over in 1902. Then for nearly seventy years the rubber-cored ball, with all sorts of different markings on the cover, was accepted as golf-ball perfection. Now we are getting back to the solid centre ball again, but unlike the entirely solid gutty it has a thin outer cover of a tough white material, making it almost indestructible and yet long flying. How long will this latest type of golf-ball construction remain popular? I feel a long time, because it gives a most satisfying click off the club face, which all golfers enjoy, particularly on the putting green.

Since the Americans Tom Weiskopf and Johnny Miller became household names in big golf, using an 'open-to-shut' technique – the opposite of the 'shut-to-open' action – allowing the club face to open as the shoulders turned on the way back from the address position, and letting the left wrist cock and stay under the shaft at the top, necessitating a strong early hit with the right hand to square up the club face on impact, this method, which I have always recommended, has become the 'in' thing once again. Now Gary Player and Arnold Palmer, for years advocates of the closed face at the top, have switched to the open club face method. They 'kill' the ball with the right hand on the way down to impact and in consequence I feel

their striking has improved. Golfers are beginning to realize that this method is in fact easier for all to use. Even the great Jack Nicklaus now recommends 'open to shut', so now it's I who have become the in' instructor once more, as I've stayed with this belief for some forty-five years.

The wheel has indeed come full circle, but it has taken nearly thirty years to vindicate the 'open to shut' at the price of demoting the 'square-to-square' method, that over-estimated, hard-to-handle system, which has ruined and injured thousands and thousands of golfers, which I always thought a crime, for golf for most is just fun and exercise.

With my explanation and demonstration of how to use the right hand and to the best advantage, I often add 20 yards to the tee shots of the 'square-to-square' or 'shut-to-open' players, giving them a feeling of freedom only comparable to taking handcuffs off a prisoner.

This fast, free hit can be best developed by hitting at an old motor-car tire outer cover lying on the ground. No other trick I have discovered sells this 'impact shock' better or builds up the golfing muscles more satisfactorily. I trained myself, before discovering this trainer, by swiping through the tallest and thickest pieces of rough grass I could find; but so many course had no rough anywhere, so I was done. Now the old tire is the answer to my dream of finding one day a perfect hand, arm and body exerciser. With it I do teaching 'miracles' every day because the impact shock which the body has to absorb anyway, is greater than that of a mere golf ball and so the various parts of the body concerned with the actual strike soon tone up for their job.

Gary Player explodes from a
bunker. The left arm shows that
he followed on after the ball, but
the angle of the shaft and the lost
grip of his right hand give an
indication of the impact involved
when a ball is trapped in deep sand

9 A Game for All

Top left A fully automated golf centre, Europe's first, opened in 1963 at Finchley, London. There were 48 automatic tees and it could theoretically accommodate 25,000 golfers a week. The use of clubs was free and the charge was one penny per shot (one cent). An average golfer might hit 40 balls in 7 mins, $2\frac{1}{2}$ times as many as with manual teeing

The game spread. South Africans (below left) seen playing in 1933. Iroquois are out on the course near Montreal (top right) in 1938, and Sheikh Abdallah (below right) tees off, watched by his sons, outside Cairo, in 1939

217

Above The Duke of York, later
King George VI, driving at
Camberley, England, 1934. Not as
keen as his brother, the Prince of
Wales, he was nevertheless the
better player
Left Douglas Bader, the Royal
Air Force hero who lost both legs
in World War II, gave much
encouragement to other disabled
people by his perseverance in
overcoming his own disability
and playing a good game of golf

Right Angel Gallardo of Spain
moves on an alligator on the 18th
fairway during the 1971 World
Cup in Florida
Below Some stunts can make
teeth rattle. Here Paul Hahn is
driving from a tee held in the
girl's teeth, 1955

Results of some championships

British Open Championship

The British Open ('The Open') is the oldest championship in golf, dating from 1860. 'The Cup' was first presented in 1872. Today competitors are limited to 120, after the qualifying rounds.

Year	Site	Winner	Runner-Up	Score
1860	Prestwick, Scotland	Willie Park, Sr	Tom Morris, Sr	174
1861	Prestwick, Scotland	Tom Morris, Sr	Willie Park, Sr	163
1862	Prestwick, Scotland	Tom Morris, Sr	Willie Park, Sr	163
1863	Prestwick, Scotland	Willie Park, Sr	Tom Morris, Sr	168
1864	Prestwick, Scotland	Tom Morris, Sr	Andrew Strath	167
1865	Prestwick, Scotland	Andrew Strath	Willie Park, Sr	162
1866	Prestwick, Scotland	Willie Park, Sr	David Park	169
1867	Prestwick, Scotland	Tom Morris, Sr	Willie Park, Sr	170
1868	Prestwick, Scotland	Tom Morris, Jr	Tom Morris, Sr	170
1869	Prestwick, Scotland	Tom Morris, Jr	Tom Morris, Sr	157
1870	Prestwick, Scotland	Tom Morris, Jr	David Strath, Robert Kirk	149
1871	Not played			
1872	Prestwick, Scotland	Tom Morris, Jr	David Strath	166
1873	St Andrews, Scotland	Tom Kidd		179
1874	Musselburgh, Scotland	Mungo Park		159
1875	Prestwick, Scotland	Willie Park, Sr	Robert Martin	166
1876	St Andrews, Scotland	Robert Martin	David Strath (refused play-off)	176
1877	Musselburgh, Scotland	Jamie Anderson	R. Pringle	160
1878	Prestwick, Scotland	Jamie Anderson	Robert Kirk	157
1879	St Andrews, Scotland	Jamie Anderson	Andrew Kirkaldy, J. Allan	170
1880	Musselburgh, Scotland	Robert Ferguson		162
1881	Prestwick, Scotland	Robert Ferguson	Jamie Anderson	170
1882	St Andrews, Scotland	Robert Ferguson	Willie Fernie	171
1883	Musselburgh, Scotland	Willie Fernie	Robert Ferguson	159
1884	Prestwick, Scotland	Jack Simpson	Douglas Rolland, Willie Fernie	160
1885	St Andrews, Scotland	Robert Martin	Archie Simpson	171
1886	Musselburgh, Scotland	David Brown	Willie Campbell	157
1887	Prestwick, Scotland	Willie Park, Jr	Robert Martin	161
1888	St Andrews, Scotland	Jack Burns	B. Sayers, D. Anderson	171
1889	Musselburgh, Scotland	Willie Park, Jr	Andrew Kirkaldy	155
1890	Prestwick, Scotland	John Ball	Willie Fernie, Archie Simpson	164
1891	St Andrews, Scotland	Hugh Kirkaldy	Andrew Kirkaldy, Willie Fernie	166
1892	Muirfield, Scotland	Harold H. Hilton	John Ball, Hugh Kirkaldy, Alexander Herd	305
1893	Prestwick, Scotland	William Auchterlonie	John Laidlay	322
1894	Sandwich, England	John H. Taylor	Douglas Rolland	326
1895	St Andrews, Scotland	John H. Taylor	Alexander Herd	322
1896	Muirfield, Scotland	Harry Vardon	John H. Taylor	316
1897	Hoylake, England	Harold H. Hilton	James Braid	314
1898	Prestwick, Scotland	Harry Vardon	Willie Park, Jr	307
1899	Sandwich, England	Harry Vardon	Jack White	310
1900	St Andrews, Scotland	John H. Taylor	Harry Vardon	309
1901	Muirfield, Scotland	James Braid	Harry Vardon	309
1902	Hoylake, England	Alexander Herd	Harry Vardon	307
1903	Prestwick, Scotland	Harry Vardon	Tom Vardon	300
1904	Sandwich, England	Jack White	John H. Taylor, James Braid	296
1905	St Andrews, Scotland	James Braid	John H. Taylor, Rolland Jones	318
1906	Muirfield, Scotland	James Braid	John H. Taylor	300
1907	Hoylake, England	Arnaud Massy	John H. Taylor	312
1908	Prestwick, Scotland	James Braid	Tom Ball	291
1909	Deal, England	John H. Taylor	James Braid, Tom Ball	295
1910	St Andrews, Scotland	James Braid	Alexander Herd	299
1911	Sandwich, England	Harry Vardon	Arnaud Massy	303
1912	Muirfield, Scotland	Edward Ray	Harry Vardon	295
1913	Hoylake, England	John H. Taylor	Edward Ray	304
1914	Prestwick, Scotland	Harry Vardon	John H. Taylor	306
1915–19	Not played			
1920	Deal, England	George Duncan	Alexander Herd	303
1921	St Andrews, Scotland	Jock Hutchison	Roger Wethered	296

1922	Sandwich, England	Walter Hagen	George Duncan, James Barnes	300
1923	Troon, Scotland	Arthur Havers	Walter Hagen	295
1924	Hoylake, England	Walter Hagen	Ernest Whitcombe	301
1925	Prestwick, Scotland	James Barnes	Archie Compston, Edward Ray	300
1926	Royal Lytham and St Anne's, England	Robert T. Jones, Jr	Al Watrous	291
1927	St Andrews, Scotland	Robert T. Jones, Jr	Aubrey Boomer	285
1928	Sandwich, England	Walter Hagen	Gene Sarazen	292
1929	Muirfield, Scotland	Walter Hagen	Johnny Farrell	292
1930	Hoylake, England	Robert T. Jones, Jr	Macdonald Smith, Leo Diegel	291
1931	Carnoustie, Scotland	Tommy Armour	J. Jurado	296
1932	Princes, England	Gene Sarazen	Macdonald Smith	283
1933	St Andrews, Scotland	Denny Shute	Craig Wood	292
1934	Sandwich, England	T. Henry Cotton	S. F. Brews	283
1935	Muirfield, Scotland	Alfred Perry	Alfred Padgham	283
1936	Hoylake, England	Alfred Padgham	J. Adams	287
1937	Carnoustie, Scotland	T. Henry Cotton	R. A. Whitcombe	290
1938	Sandwich, England	R. A. Whitcombe	James Adams	295
1939	St Andrews, Scotland	Richard Burton	Johnny Bulla	290
1940–45	Not played			
1946	St Andrews, Scotland	Sam Snead	A. D. Locke, Johnny Bulla	290
1947	Hoylake, England	Fred Daly	R. W. Horne, Frank Stranahan	293
1948	Muirfield, Scotland	T. Henry Cotton	Fred Daly	284
1949	Sandwich, England	A. D. Locke	Harry Bradshaw	283
1950	Troon, Scotland	A. D. Locke	Roberto DeVicenzo	279
1951	Portrush, Northern Ireland	Max Faulkner	A. Cerda	285
1952	Royal Lytham and St Anne's, England	A. D. Locke	Peter W. Thomson	287
1953	Carnoustie, Scotland	Ben Hogan	Frank Stranahan, Dai Rees, Peter W. Thomson, A. Cerda	282
1954	Royal Birkdale, England	Peter W. Thomson	S. S. Scott, Dai Rees, A. D. Locke	283
1955	St Andrews, Scotland	Peter W. Thomson	John Fallon	281
1956	Hoylake, England	Peter W. Thomson	Flory VanDonck	286
1957	St Andrews, Scotland	A. D. Locke	Peter W. Thomson	279
1958	Royal Lytham and St Anne's, England	Peter W. Thomson	Dave Thomas	278
1959	Muirfield, Scotland	Gary Player	Flory VanDonck	284
1960	St Andrews, Scotland	K. D. G. Nagle	Arnold Palmer	278
1961	Royal Birkdale, England	Arnold Palmer	Dai Rees	284
1962	Troon, Scotland	Arnold Palmer	K. D. G. Nagle	276
1963	Royal Lytham and St Anne's, England	Robert J. Charles	Phil Rodgers	277
1964	St Andrews, Scotland	Tony Lema	Jack Nicklaus	279
1965	Southport, England	Peter W. Thomson	B. G. C. Huggett, Chris O'Connor	285
1966	Muirfield, Scotland	Jack Nicklaus	Doug Sanders, Dave Thomas	282
1967	Hoylake, England	Robert DeVicenzo	Jack Nicklaus	278
1968	Carnoustie, Scotland	Gary Player	Jack Nicklaus, Robert J. Charles	289
1969	Royal Lytham and St Anne's, England	Tony Jacklin	Robert J. Charles	280
1970	St Andrews, Scotland	Jack Nicklaus	Doug Sanders	283
1971	Southport, England	Lee Trevino	Liang Huan Lu	278
1972	Muirfield, Scotland	Lee Trevino	Jack Nicklaus	278
1973	Troon, Scotland	Tom Weiskopf	Neil Coles, Johnny Miller	276
1974	Royal Lytham and St Anne's, England	Gary Player	Peter Oosterhuis	282

United States National Open Championship

Inaugurated on the 9-hole course at Newport Golf Club (RI) in 1895. After a series of qualifying rounds (from which many players are exempt by reason of past successes), the final field is limited to 150 players.

Year	Site	Winner	Runner-up	Score
1895	Newport GC, Newport, RI	Horace Rawlins	Willie Dunn	173
1896	Shinnecock Hills GC, Southampton, NY	James Foulis	Horace Rawlins	152
1897	Chicago GC, Wheaton, Ill.	Joe Lloyd	Willie Anderson	162
1898	Myopia Hunt Club, Hamilton, Mass.	Fred Herd	Alex Smith	328
1899	Baltimore CC, Baltimore, Md	Willie Smith	George Low, Val Fitzjohn, W. H. Way	315
1900	Chicago GC, Wheaton, Ill.	Harry Vardon	J. H. Taylor	313
1901	Myopia Hunt Club, Hamilton, Mass.	Willie Anderson	Alex Smith	331–85
1902	Garden City GC, Garden City, NY	L. Auchterlonie	Stewart Gardner, W. J. Travis	307

1903	Baltusrol GC, Springfield, NJ	Willie Anderson	David Brown	307–82
1904	Glen View Club, Golf, Ill.	Willie Anderson	Gil Nicholls	303
1905	Myopia Hunt Club, Hamilton, Mass.	Willie Anderson	Alex Smith	314
1906	Onwentsia Club, Lake Forest, Ill.	Alex Smith	William Smith	295
1907	Philadelphia Cricket Club, Philadelphia, Pa	Alex Ross	Gil Nicholls	302
1908	Myopia Hunt Club, Hamilton, Mass.	Fred McLeod	Willie Smith	322–77
1909	Englewood GC, Englewood, NJ	George Sargent	Tom McNamara	290
1910	Philadelphia Cricket Club, St Martins, Pa	Alex Smith	John J. McDermott, Macdonald Smith	298–71
1911	Chicago GC, Wheaton, Ill.	John J. McDermott	Michael J. Brady, George O. Simpson	307–80
1912	CC of Buffalo, Buffalo, NY	John J. McDermott	Tom McNamara	294
1913	The Country Club, Brookline, Mass.	Francis Ouimet	Harry Vardon, Edward Ray	304–72
1914	Midlothian CC, Blue Island, Ill.	Walter Hagen	Charles Evans, Jr	290
1915	Baltusrol GC, Springfield, NJ	Jerome D. Travers	Tom McNamara	297
1916	Minikahda Club, Minneapolis, Minn.	Charles Evans, Jr	Jock Hutchison	286
1917–18	Not played			
1919	Brae Burn CC, West Newton, Mass.	Walter Hagen	Michael J. Brady	301–77
1920	Inverness Club, Toledo, Ohio	Edward Ray	Harry Vardon, Jack Burke, Leo Diegel, Jock Hutchison	295
1921	Columbia CC, Chevy Chase, Md	James M. Barnes	Walter Hagen, Fred McLeod	289
1922	Skokie CC, Glencoe, Ill.	Gene Sarazen	Robert T. Jones, Jr John L. Black	288
1923	Inwood CC, Inwood, NY	Robert T. Jones, Jr	Robert A. Cruickshank	296–76
1924	Oakland Hills CC, Birmingham, Mich.	Cyril Walker	Robert T. Jones, Jr	297
1925	Worcester CC, Worcester, Mass.	William Macfarlane	Robert T. Jones, Jr	291–75–72
1926	Scioto CC, Columbus, Ohio	Robert T. Jones, Jr	Joe Turnesa	293
1927	Oakmont CC, Oakmont, Pa	Tommy Armour	Harry Cooper	301–76
1928	Olympia Fields CC, Matteson, Ill.	Johnny Farrell	Robert T. Jones, Jr	294–143
1929	Winged Foot GC, Mamaroneck, NY	Robert T. Jones, Jr	Al Espinosa	294–141
1930	Interlachen CC, Minneapolis, Minn.	Robert T. Jones, Jr	Macdonald Smith	287
1931	Inverness Club, Toledo, Ohio	Billy Burke	George Von Elm	292–149–148
1932	Fresh Meadow, Flushing, NY	Gene Sarazen	Robert A. Cruickshank, T. Philip Perkins	286
1933	North Shore GC, Glen View, Ill.	John G. Goodman	Ralph Guldahl	287
1934	Merion Cricket Club, Ardmore, Pa	Olin Dutra	Gene Sarazen	293
1935	Oakmont CC, Oakmont, Pa	Sam Parks, Jr	Jimmy Thomson	299
1936	Baltusrol GC, Springfield, NJ	Tony Manero	Harry E. Cooper	282
1937	Oakland Hills CC, Birmingham, Mich.	Ralph Guldahl	Sam Snead	281
1938	Cherry Hills Club, Denver, Colo	Ralph Guldahl	Dick Metz	284
1939	Philadelphia CC, West Conshohocken, Pa	Byron Nelson	Craig Wood, Denny Shute	284–68–70
1940	Canterbury GC, Cleveland, Ohio	Lawson Little	Gene Sarazen	287–70
1941	Colonial Club, Fort Worth, Texas	Craig Wood	Denny Shute	284
1942–45	Not played			
1946	Canterbury GC, Cleveland, Ohio	Lloyd Mangrum	Byron Nelson, Victor Ghezzi	284–72–72
1947	St Louis CC, Clayton, Mo.	Lew Worsham	Sam Snead	282–69
1948	Riviera CC, Los Angeles, Calif.	Ben Hogan	Jimmy Demaret	276
1949	Medinah CC, Medinah, Ill.	Cary Middlecoff	Sam Snead, Clayton Heafner	286
1950	Merion GC, Ardmore, Pa	Ben Hogan	Lloyd Mangrum, George Fazio	287–69
1951	Oakland Hills CC, Birmingham, Mich.	Ben Hogan	Clayton Heafner	287
1952	Northwood Club, Dallas, Texas	Julius Boros	Edward S. Oliver, Jr	281
1953	Oakmont CC, Oakmont, Pa	Ben Hogan	Sam Snead	283
1954	Baltusrol GC, Springfield, NJ	Ed Furgol	Gene Littler	284
1955	Olympic CC, San Francisco, Calif.	Jack Fleck	Ben Hogan	287–69
1956	Oak Hill CC, Rochester, NY	Cary Middlecoff	Julius Boros, Ben Hogan	281
1957	Inverness Club, Toledo, Ohio	Dick Mayer	Cary Middlecoff	282–72
1958	Southern Hills CC, Tulsa, Okla	Tommy Bolt	Gary Player	283
1959	Winged Foot CC, Mamaroneck, NY	Billy Casper, Jr	Robert R. Rosburg	282
1960	Cherry Hills CC, Englewood, Colo	Arnold Palmer	Jack Nicklaus	280
1961	Oakland Hills CC, Birmingham, Mich.	Gene Littler	Bob Goalby, Doug Sanders	281
1962	Oakmont CC, Oakmont, Pa	Jack Nicklaus	Arnold Palmer	283–71
1963	The Country Club, Brookline, Mass.	Julius Boros	Jacky Cupit, Arnold Palmer	293–70
1964	Congressional CC, Washington, DC	Ken Venturi	Tommy Jacobs	278
1965	Bellerive CC, St Louis, Mo.	Gary Player	Kel Nagle	282–71

1966	Olympic CC, San Francisco, Calif.	Billy Casper, Jr	Arnold Palmer	278–69
1967	Baltusrol GC, Springfield, NJ	Jack Nicklaus	Arnold Palmer	275
1968	Oak Hill CC, Rochester, NY	Lee B. Trevino	Jack Nicklaus	275
1969	Champions GC, Houston, Texas	Orville Moody	Deane Beman, Al Geiberger, Robert R. Rosburg	281
1970	Hazeltine National GC, Chaska, Minn.	Tony Jacklin	Dave Hill	281
1971	Merion GC, Ardmore, Pa	Lee B. Trevino	Jack Nicklaus	280–68
1972	Pebble Beach Golf Links, Monterey, Calif.	Jack Nicklaus	Bruce Crampton	290
1973	Oakmont CC, Oakmont, Pa	Johnny Miller	John Schlee	279
1974	Winged Foot CC, Mamoroneck, NY	Hale Irwin	Forrest Fezler	287

PGA Championship (USA)

Inaugurated in 1916, at the Siwanoy Country Club, NY, the Championship was decided by match play until 1957. Since then it has been changed to stroke play (72 holes). The field is selected from the champions of specified tournaments and other players as laid down in the rules. The rest of the field is made up from the top 70 money winners in tour events over the previous year. The total competing is around 144.

Year	Site	Winner	Runner-Up	Score
1916	Siwanoy CC, Bronxville, NY	James M. Barnes	Jock Hutchison	1 up
1917–18	Not played			
1919	Engineers CC, Roslyn, NY	James M. Barnes	Fred McLeod	6 & 5
1920	Flossmoor CC, Flossmoor, Ill.	Jock Hutchison	J. Douglas Edgar	1 up
1921	Inwood CC, Inwood, NY	Walter Hagen	James M. Barnes	3 & 2
1922	Oakmont CC, Oakmont, Pa	Gene Sarazen	Emmet French	4 & 3
1923	Pelham CC, Pelham, NY	Gene Sarazen	Walter Hagen	1 up (38)
1924	French Lick CC, French Lick, Ind.	Walter Hagen	James M. Barnes	2 up
1925	Olympia Fields CC, Olympia, Ill.	Walter Hagen	Wm. Mehlhorn	6 & 5
1926	Salisbury GC, Westbury, LI, NY	Walter Hagen	Leo Diegel	5 & 3
1927	Cedar Crest CC, Dallas, Texas	Walter Hagen	Joe Turnesa	1 up
1928	Baltimore CC, Five Farms, Baltimore, Md	Leo Diegel	Al Espinosa	6 & 5
1929	Hillcrest CC, Los Angeles, Calif.	Leo Diegel	Johnny Farrell	6 & 4
1930	Fresh Meadow, Flushing, NY	Tommy Armour	Gene Sarazen	1 up
1931	Wannamoisett CC, Rumford, RI	Tom Creavy	Denny Shute	2 & 1
1932	Keller GC, St Paul, Minn.	Olin Dutra	Frank Walsh	4 & 3
1933	Blue Mound CC, Milwaukee, Wis.	Gene Sarazen	Willie Goggin	5 & 4
1934	Park CC, Williamsville, NY	Paul Runyan	Craig Wood	1 up (38)
1935	Twin Hills CC, Oklahoma City, Okla	John Revolta	Tommy Armour	5 & 4
1936	Pinehurst CC, Pinehurst, NC	Denny Shute	Jimmy Thomson	3 & 2
1937	Pittsburgh CC, Aspinwall, Pa	Denny Shute	Harold McSpaden	1 up (37)
1938	Shawnee CC, Shawnee-on-Dela., Pa	Paul Runyan	Sam Snead	8 & 7
1939	Pomonok CC, Flushing, NY	Henry Picard	Byron Nelson	1 up (37)
1940	Hershey CC, Hershey, Pa	Byron Nelson	Sam Snead	1 up
1941	Cherry Hills CC, Denver, Colo	Vic Ghezzi	Byron Nelson	1 up (38)
1942	Seaview CC, Atlantic City, NJ	Sam Snead	Jim Turnesa	2 & 1
1943	Not played			
1944	Manito G & CC, Spokane, Wash.	Bob Hamilton	Byron Nelson	1 up
1945	Morraine CC, Dayton, Ohio	Byron Nelson	Sam Byrd	4 & 3
1946	Portland GC, Portland, Ore.	Ben Hogan	Ed Oliver	6 & 4
1947	Plum Hollow CC, Detroit, Mich.	Jim Ferrier	Chick Harbert	2 & 1
1948	Norwood Hills CC, St Louis, Mo.	Ben Hogan	Mike Turnesa	7 & 6
1949	Hermitage CC, Richmond, Va	Sam Snead	Johnny Palmer	3 & 2
1950	Scioto CC, Columbus, Ohio	Chandler Harper	H. Williams, Jr	4 & 3
1951	Oakmont CC, Oakmont, Pa	Sam Snead	Walter Burkemo	7 & 6
1952	Big Spring CC, Louisville, Ky	Jim Turnesa	Chick Harbert	1 up
1953	Birmingham CC, Birmingham, Mich.	Walter Burkemo	Felice Torza	2 & 1
1954	Keller GC, St Paul, Minn.	Chick Harbert	Walter Burkemo	4 & 3
1955	Meadowbrook CC, Detroit, Mich.	Doug Ford	Cary Middlecoff	4 & 3
1956	Blue Hill CC, Boston, Mass.	Jack Burke, Jr	Ted Kroll	3 & 2
1957	Miami Valley GC, Dayton, Ohio	Lionel Hebert	Dow Finsterwald	2 & 1
1958	Llanerch CC, Havertown, Pa	Dow Finsterwald	Billy Casper, Jr	276
1959	Minneapolis GC, St Louis, Minn.	Bob Rosburg	Jerry Barber, Doug Sanders	277
1960	Firestone CC, Akron, Ohio	Jay Hebert	Jim Ferrier	281
1961	Olympia Fields CC, Olympia, Ill.	Jerry Barber	Don January	277
1962	Aronimink GC, Newtown Sq., Pa	Gary Player	Bob Goalby	278

1963	Dallas Athletic Club GC, Dallas, Texas	Jack Nicklaus	Dave Ragan, Jr	279
1964	Columbus CC, Columbus, Ohio	Bob Nichols	Jack Nicklaus, Arnold Palmer	271
1965	Laurel Valley GC, Ligonier, Pa	Dave Marr	Jack Nicklaus, Billy Casper, Jr	280
1966	Firestone CC, Akron, Ohio	Al Geiberger	Dudley Wysong	280
1967	Columbine CC, Denver, Colo	Don January	Don Massengale	281
1968	Pecan Valley CC, San Antonio, Texas	Julius Boros	Robert J. Charles	281
1969	National Cash Register CC, Dayton, Ohio	Ray Floyd	Gary Player	276
1970	Southern Hills CC, Tulsa, Okla	Dave Stockton	Bob Murphy, Arnold Palmer	279
1971	PGA National GC, Palm Beach Gardens, Fla	Jack Nicklaus	Billy Casper	281
1972	Oakland Hills CC, Birmingham, Mich.	Gary Player	Jim Jamieson	281
1973	Canterbury GC, Cleveland, Ohio	Jack Nicklaus	Bruce Crampton	277
1974	Clemmons CC, NC	Lee Trevino	Jack Nicklaus	276

The Masters Tournament

Always played at the Augusta National Golf Club, Ga, the Masters has been strictly an invitation tournament since its inception in 1934. The initial field of about 90 players is reduced to 40 for the last two rounds.

Year	Winner	Runner-Up	Score	Year	Winner	Runner-Up	Score
1934	Horton Smith	Craig Wood	284	1959	Art Wall, Jr	Fred Hawkins	284
1935	Gene Sarazen	Craig Wood	282	1960	Arnold Palmer	Ken Venturi	282
1936	Horton Smith	Harry Cooper	285	1961	Gary Player	Arnold Palmer, Charles Coe	280
1937	Byron Nelson	Ralph Guldahl	283				
1938	Henry Picard	Ralph Guldahl	285	1962	Arnold Palmer	Gary Player, Dow Finsterwald	280
1939	Ralph Guldahl	Sam Snead	279				
1940	Jimmy Demaret	Lloyd Mangrum	280	1963	Jack Nicklaus	Tony Lema	286
1941	Craig Wood	Byron Nelson	280	1964	Arnold Palmer	Dave Marr, Jack Nicklaus	276
1942	Byron Nelson	Ben Hogan	280	1965	Jack Nicklaus	Arnold Palmer, Gary Player	271
1943–45	Not played						
1946	Herman Keiser	Ben Hogan	282	1966	Jack Nicklaus	Tommy Jacobs, Gay Brewer, Jr	288
1947	Jimmy Demaret	Byron Nelson	281				
1948	Claude Harmon	Cary Middlecoff	279	1967	Gay Brewer, Jr	Bob Nichols	280
1949	Sam Snead	Lloyd Mangrum, Johnny Bulla	282	1968	Bob Goalby	Roberto DeVicenzo	277
				1969	George Archer	Billy Casper, Jr, George Knudson, Tom Weiskopf	281
1950	Jimmy Demaret	Jim Ferrier	283				
1951	Ben Hogan	Robert Riegel	280				
1952	Sam Snead	Jack Burke, Jr	286	1970	Billy Casper, Jr	Gene Littler	279
1953	Ben Hogan	Ed Oliver	274	1971	Charles Coody	John Miller, Jack Nicklaus	279
1954	Sam Snead	Ben Hogan	289	1972	Jack Nicklaus	Bruce Crampton, Tom Weiskopf, Bobby Mitchell	286
1955	Cary Middlecoff	Ben Hogan	279				
1956	Jack Burke, Jr	Ken Venturi	289				
1957	Doug Ford	Sam Snead	283	1973	Tommy Aaron	J. C. Snead	283
1958	Arnold Palmer	Doug Ford	284	1974	Gary Player	Dave Stockton, Tom Weiskopf	278

Piccadilly World Match-Play Championship

The brain-child of Mark H. McCormack, representative for many of the leading golfers in the world, this is a 36-hole match-play event, among the eight leading golfers of the year. It is always played at the Wentworth Club, Surrey, England. Automatic invitations go to the defending champion, and the winners of the British and US Opens, the Masters and the British PGA Match Play.

Year	Winner	Runner-Up	Score
1964	Arnold Palmer	Neil Coles	2 & 1
1965	Gary Player	Peter Thomson	3 & 2
1966	Gary Player	Jack Nicklaus	6 & 4
1967	Arnold Palmer	Peter Thomson	2 up
1968	Gary Player	Robert J. Charles	1 up
1969	Robert J. Charles	Gene Littler	1 up (37 holes)
1970	Jack Nicklaus	Lee Trevino	2 & 1
1971	Gary Player	Jack Nicklaus	5 & 4
1972	Tom Weiskopf	Lee Trevino	4 & 3
1973	Gary Player	Graham Marsh	1 up (40 holes)
1974	Hale Irwin	Gary Player	2 & 1

British Amateur Championship

A match-play championship since its informal beginnings at the Royal Liverpool Club, Hoylake, in 1885. The quarter- and semi-finals and the final are decided over 36 holes.

Year	Site	Winner	Runner-Up	Score
1887	Hoylake, England	H. G. Hutchinson	John Ball	1 up
1888	Prestwick, Scotland	John Ball	J. E. Laidlay	5 & 4
1889	St Andrews, Scotland	J. E. Laidlay	L. M. B. Melville	2 & 1
1890	Hoylake, England	John Ball	J. E. Laidlay	4 & 3
1891	St Andrews, Scotland	J. E. Laidlay	H. H. Hilton	20th hole
1892	Sandwich, England	John Ball	H. H. Hilton	3 & 1
1893	Prestwick, Scotland	Peter Anderson	J. E. Laidlay	1 up
1894	Hoylake, England	John Ball	S. M. Fergusson	1 up
1895	St Andrews, Scotland	L. M. B. Melville	John Ball	19th hole
1896	Sandwich, England	F. G. Tait	H. H. Hilton	8 & 9
1897	Muirfield, Scotland	A. J. T. Allan	James Robb	4 & 2
1898	Hoylake, England	F. G. Tait	S. M. Fergusson	7 & 5
1899	Prestwick, Scotland	John Ball	F. G. Tait	37th hole
1900	Sandwich, England	H. H. Hilton	James Robb	8 & 7
1901	St Andrews, Scotland	H. H. Hilton	J. L. Low	1 up
1902	Hoylake, England	C. Hutchings	S. H. Fry	1 up
1903	Muirfield, Scotland	R. Maxwell	H. G. Hutchinson	7 & 5
1904	Sandwich, England	W. J. Travis	Edward Blackwell	4 & 3
1905	Prestwick, Scotland	A. G. Barry	O. Scott	3 & 2
1906	Hoylake, England	James Robb	C. C. Lingen	4 & 3
1907	St Andrews, Scotland	John Ball	C. A. Palmer	6 & 4
1908	Sandwich, England	E. A. Lassen	H. E. Taylor	7 & 6
1909	Muirfield, Scotland	R. Maxwell	Capt. C. K. Hutchinson	1 up
1910	Hoylake, England	John Ball	C. Aylmer	10 & 9
1911	Prestwick, Scotland	H. H. Hilton	E. A. Lassen	4 & 3
1912	Westward Ho!, England	John Ball	Abe Mitchell	38th hole
1913	St Andrews, Scotland	H. H. Hilton	R. Harris	6 & 5
1914	Sandwich, England	J. L. C. Jenkins	C. O. Hezlet	3 & 2
1915–19 Not played				
1920	Muirfield, Scotland	C. J. H. Tolley	R. A. Gardner	37th hole
1921	Hoylake, England	W. I. Hunter	A. J. Graham	12 & 11
1922	Prestwick, Scotland	E. W. E. Holderness	J. Caven	1 up
1923	Deal, England	R. H. Wethered	R. Harris	7 & 6
1924	St Andrews, Scotland	E. W. E. Holderness	E. F. Storey	3 & 2
1925	Westward Ho!, England	R. Harris	K. F. Fradgley	13 & 12
1926	Muirfield, Scotland	Jess Sweetser	A. F. Simpson	6 & 5
1927	Hoylake, England	Dr W. Tweddell	D. E. Landale	7 & 6
1928	Prestwick, Scotland	T. P. Perkins	R. H. Wethered	6 & 4
1929	Sandwich, England	C. J. H. Tolley	J. N. Smith	4 & 3
1930	St Andrews, Scotland	Robert T. Jones, Jr	R. H. Wethered	7 & 6
1931	Westward Ho!, England	E. Martin Smith	J. DeForest	1 up
1932	Muirfield, Scotland	J. DeForest	E. W. Fiddian	3 & 1
1933	Hoylake, England	M. Scott	T. A. Bourn	4 & 3
1934	Prestwick, Scotland	W. Lawson Little	J. Wallace	14 & 13
1935	Royal Lytham and St Anne's, England	W. Lawson Little	Dr W. Tweddell	1 up
1936	St Andrews, Scotland	H. Thomson	J. Ferrier	2 up
1937	Sandwich, England	R. Sweeny, Jr	L. O. Munn	3 & 2
1938	Troon, Scotland	C. R. Yates	R. C. Ewing	3 & 2
1939	Hoylake, England	A. T. Kyle	A. A. Duncan	2 & 1
1940–45 Not played				
1946	Royal Birkdale, England	J. Bruen	R. Sweeny, Jr	4 & 3
1947	Carnoustie, Scotland	Willie D. Turnesa	R. D. Chapman	3 & 2
1948	Sandwich, England	Frank R. Stranahan	C. Stowe	5 & 4
1949	Portmarnock, Ireland	S. M. McCready	W. P. Turnesa	2 & 1
1950	St Andrews, Scotland	Frank R. Stranahan	R. D. Chapman	3 & 6
1951	Porthcawl, South Wales	Richard D. Chapman	C. R. Coe	5 & 4
1952	Prestwick, Scotland	E. H. Ward	F. R. Stranahan	6 & 5
1953	Hoylake, England	J. B. Carr	E. Harvie Ward	2 up
1954	Muirfield, Scotland	D. W. Bachli	W. C. Campbell	2 & 1

1955	Royal Lytham and St Anne's, England	J. W. Conrad	A. Slater	3 & 2
1956	Troon, Scotland	J. C. Beharrel	L. G. Taylor	5 & 4
1957	Formby, England	R. Reid Jack	H. B. Ridgley	2 & 1
1958	St Andrews, Scotland	J. B. Carr	A. Thirlwell	3 & 2
1959	Sandwich, England	Deane Beman	William Hyndman III	3 & 2
1960	Portrush, Northern Ireland	J. B. Carr	R. Cochran	7 & 6
1961	Turnberry, Scotland	M. Bonallack	J. Walker	6 & 4
1962	Hoylake, England	R. Davies	J. Powell	1 up
1963	St Andrews, Scotland	M. Lunt	J. Blackwell	2 & 1
1964	Ganton, England	C. Clark	M. Lunt	1 up (39)
1965	Porthcawl, South Wales	M. Bonallack	C. Clark	2 & 1
1966	Carnoustie, Scotland	C. R. Cole	R. Shade	3 & 2
1967	Formby, England	R. Dickson	R. Cerrudo	2 & 1
1968	Troon, Scotland	M. Bonallack	J. B. Carr	7 & 6
1969	Hoylake, England	M. Bonallack	William Hyndman III	3 & 2
1970	Hoylake, England	M. Bonallack	William Hyndman III	8 & 7
1971	Newcastle Co. Down, Northern Ireland	Steve Melnyk	Jim Simons	3 & 2
1972	Sandwich, England	Trevor Homer	Alan Thirlwell	4 & 3
1973	Porthcawl, South Wales	R. Siderowf	P. Moody	5 & 3
1974	Muirfield, Scotland	Trevor Homer	J. Gabrielsen	2 up

United States National Amateur Championship

First played in 1895 at Newport Golf Club (RI), it remained a match-play championship until 1964, since when it became a 72-hole stroke-play event until 1973.

Year	Site	Winner	Runner-Up	Score
1895	Newport GC, Newport, RI	Charles B. Macdonald	Charles E. Sands	12 & 11
1896	Shinnecock Hills GC, Southampton, NY	H. J. Whigham	J. G. Thorp	8 & 7
1897	Chicago GC, Wheaton, Ill.	H. J. Whigham	W. Rossiter Betts	8 & 6
1898	Morris County GC, Morristown, NJ	Findlay S. Douglas	Walter B. Smith	5 & 3
1899	Onwentsia Club, Lake Forest, Ill.	H. M. Harriman	Findlay S. Douglas	3 & 2
1900	Garden City GC, Garden City, NY	Walter J. Travis	Findlay S. Douglas	2 up
1901	CC of Atlantic City, Atlantic City, NJ	Walter J. Travis	Walter E. Egan	5 & 4
1902	Glen View Club, Golf, Ill.	Louis N. James	Eben M. Byers	4 & 2
1903	Nassau CC, Glen Cove, NY	Walter J. Travis	Eben M. Byers	5 & 4
1904	Baltusrol GC, Springfield, NJ	H. Chandler Egan	Fred Herreshoff	8 & 6
1905	Chicago GC, Wheaton, Ill.	H. Chandler Egan	D. E. Sawyer	6 & 5
1906	Englewood GC, Englewood, NJ	Eben M. Byers	George S. Lyon	2 up
1907	Euclid Club, Cleveland, Ohio	Jerome D. Travers	Archibald Graham	6 & 5
1908	Garden City GC, Garden City, NY	Jerome D. Travers	Max H. Behr	8 & 7
1909	Chicago GC, Wheaton, Ill.	Robert A. Gardner	H. Chandler Egan	4 & 3
1910	The Country Club, Brookline, Mass.	William C. Fownes, Jr	Warren K. Wood	4 & 3
1911	The Apawamis Club, Rye, NY	Harold H. Hilton	Fred Herreshoff	1 up, 37 holes
1912	Chicago GC, Wheaton, Ill.	Jerome D. Travers	Charles Evans, Jr	7 & 6
1913	Garden City GC, Garden City, NY	Jerome D. Travers	John G. Anderson	5 & 4
1914	Ekwanok CC, Manchester, Vt	Francis Ouimet	Jerome D. Travers	6 & 5
1915	CC of Detroit, Grosse Pointe Farms, Mich.	Robert A. Gardner	John G. Anderson	5 & 4
1916	Merion Cricket Club, Haverford, Pa	Charles Evans, Jr	Robert A. Gardner	4 & 3
1917–18	Not played			
1919	Oakmont CC, Oakmont, Pa	S. Davidson Herron	Robert T. Jones, Jr	5 & 4
1920	Engineers CC, Roslyn, NY	Charles Evans, Jr	Francis Ouimet	7 & 6
1921	St Louis CC, Clayton, Mo.	Jesse P. Guilford	Robert A. Gardner	7 & 6
1922	The Country Club, Brookline, Mass.	Jess W. Sweetser	Charles Evans, Jr	3 & 2
1923	Flossmoor CC, Flossmoor, Ill.	Max R. Marston	Jess W. Sweetser	1 up, 38 holes
1924	Merion Cricket Club, Haverford, Pa	Robert T. Jones, Jr	George Von Elm	9 & 8
1925	Oakmont CC, Oakmont, Pa	Robert T. Jones, Jr	Watts Gunn	8 & 7
1926	Baltusrol GC, Springfield, NJ	George Von Elm	Robert T. Jones, Jr	2 & 1
1927	Minikahda Club, Minneapolis, Minn.	Robert T. Jones, Jr	Charles Evans, Jr	8 & 7
1928	Brae Burn CC, West Newton, Mass.	Robert T. Jones, Jr	T. Philip Perkins	10 & 9
1929	Del Monte G & CC, Pebble Beach Course, Calif.	Harrison R. Johnston	Dr O. F. Willing	4 & 3
1930	Merion Cricket Club, Ardmore, Pa	Robert T. Jones, Jr	Eugene V. Homans	8 & 7
1931	Beverly CC, Chicago, Ill.	Francis Ouimet	Jack Westland	6 & 5
1932	Baltimore CC, Five Farms Course, Md	C. Ross Somerville	John Goodman	2 & 1

1933	Kenwood CC, Cincinnati, Ohio	George T. Dunlap, Jr	Max R. Marston	6 & 5
1934	The Country Club, Brookline, Mass.	W. Lawson Little, Jr	David Goldman	8 & 7
1935	The Country Club, Cleveland, Ohio	W. Lawson Little, Jr	Walter Emery	4 & 2
1936	Garden City GC, Garden City, NY	John W. Fischer	Jack McLean	1 up, 37 holes
1937	Alderwood CC, Portland, Ore.	John G. Goodman	Raymond E. Billows	2 up
1938	Oakmont CC, Oakmont, Pa	William P. Turnesa	B. Patrick Abbott	8 & 7
1939	North Shore CC, Glenview, Ill.	Marvin H. Ward	Raymond E. Billows	7 & 5
1940	Winged Foot GC, Mamaroneck, NY	Richard D. Chapman	W. B. McCullough, Jr	11 & 9
1941	Omaha Field Club, Omaha, Neb.	Marvin H. Ward	B. Patrick Abbott	4 & 3
1942–45	Not played			
1946	Baltusrol GC, Springfield, NJ	S. E. (Ted) Bishop	Smiley L. Quick	1 up, 37 holes
1947	Del Monte G & CC, Pebble Beach Course, Calif.	R. H. (Skee) Riegel	John W. Dawson	2 & 1
1948	Memphis CC, Memphis, Tenn.	William P. Turnesa	Raymond E. Billows	2 & 1
1949	Oak Hill CC, Rochester, NY	Charles R. Coe	Rufus King	11 & 10
1950	Minneapolis GC, Minneapolis, Minn.	Sam Urzetta	Frank Stranahan	1 up, 39 holes
1951	Saucon Valley CC, Bethlehem, Pa	Billy Maxwell	Joseph F. Gagliardi	4 & 3
1952	Seattle GC, Seattle, Wash.	Jack Westland	Al Mengert	3 & 2
1953	Oklahoma City G & CC, Oklahoma City, Okla	Gene A. Littler	Dale Morey	1 up
1954	CC of Detroit, Grosse Pointe Farms, Mich.	Arnold D. Palmer	Robert Sweeny	1 up
1955	CC of Virginia, Richmond, Va	E. Harvie Ward, Jr	Wm. Hyndman, III	9 & 8
1956	Knollwood Club, Lake Forest, Ill.	E. Harvie Ward, Jr	Charles Kocsis	5 & 4
1957	The Country Club, Brookline, Mass.	Hillman Robbins, Jr	Dr Frank M. Taylor	5 & 4
1958	Olympic CC, San Francisco, Calif.	Charles R. Coe	Thomas D. Aaron	5 & 4
1959	Broadmoor GC, Colorado Springs, Colo	Jack N. Nicklaus	Charles R. Coe	1 up
1960	St Louis CC, Clayton, Mo.	Deane R. Beman	Robert W. Gardner	6 & 4
1961	Pebble Beach Golf Links, Pebble Beach, Calif.	Jack W. Nicklaus	H. Dudley Wysong, Jr	8 & 6
1962	Pinehurst CC, Pinehurst, NC	Labron E. Harris, Jr	Downing Gray	1 up
1963	Wakonda Club, Des Moines, Iowa	Deane R. Beman	R. H. Sikes	2 & 1
1964	Canterbury GC, Cleveland, Ohio	William C. Campbell	Edgar M. Tutwiler	1 up
1965	Southern Hills CC, Tulsa, Okla	Robert J. Murphy, Jr	Robert B. Dickson	291
1966	Merion GC, Ardmore, Pa	Gary Cowan	Deane R. Beman	285–75
1967	Broadmoor GC, Colorado Springs, Colo	Robert B. Dickson	Marvin M. Giles, III	285
1968	Scioto CC, Columbus, Ohio	Bruce Fleisher	Marvin M. Giles, III	284
1969	Oakmont CC, Oakmont, Pa	Steve Melnyk	Marvin M. Giles, III	286
1970	Waverley CC, Portland, Ore.	Lanny Wadkins	Thomas O. Kite, Jr	279
1971	Wilmington CC, Wilmington, Del.	Gary Cowan	Eddie Pearce	280
1972	Charlotte CC, Charlotte, NC	Marvin M. Giles, III	Ben Crenshaw, Mark Hayes	285
1973	Inverness Club, Toledo, Ohio	Craig Stadler	David Strawn	6 & 5
1974	Ridgewood CC, NJ	Jerome Pate	John Grace	2 & 1

USGA Women's Amateur Championship

First played at the Meadow Brook Club, Westbury, NY, 1895, today there are two 18-hole qualifying stroke-play rounds, from which the 32 players with the lowest scores over the 36-holes go on to match play. The final round is 36 holes.

Year	Site	Winner	Runner-Up	Score
1895	Meadowbrook GC, Hempstead, NY	Mrs Charles S. Brown	N. C. Sargent	132
1896	Morris County GC, Morristown, NJ	Beatrix Hoyt	Mrs Arthur Turnure	2 & 1
1897	Essex CC, Manchester, Mass.	Beatrix Hoyt	N. C. Sargent	5 & 4
1898	Ardsley GC, Ardsley-on-the-Hudson, NY	Beatrix Hoyt	Maud Wetmore	5 & 3
1899	Philadelphia CC, Philadelphia, Pa	Ruth Underhill	Mrs Caleb Fox	2 & 1
1900	Shinnecock Hills, GC, Southampton, NY	Frances C. Griscom	Margaret Curtis	6 & 5
1901	Baltusrol GC, Springfield, NJ	Genevieve Hecker	Lucy Herron	5 & 3
1902	The Country Club, Brookline, Mass.	Genevieve Hecker	Louisa A. Wells	4 & 3
1903	Chicago GC, Wheaton, Ill.	Bessie Anthony	J. A. Carpenter	7 & 6
1904	Merion Cricket Club, Ardmore, Pa	Georgianna M. Bishop	Mrs E. F. Sanford	5 & 3
1905	Morris County GC, Morristown, NJ	Pauline Mackay	Margaret Curtis	1 up
1906	Brae Burn CC, West Newton, Mass.	Harriot S. Curtis	Mary B. Adams	2 & 1
1907	Midlothian CC, Blue Island, Ill.	Margaret Curtis	Harriot S. Curtis	7 & 6
1908	Chevy Chase Club, Chevy Chase, Md	Katherine C. Harley	Mrs T. H. Polhemus	6 & 5
1909	Merion Cricket Club, Haverford, Pa	Dorothy I. Campbell	Mrs R. H. Barlow	3 & 2

Year	Venue		Winner	Runner-up	Score
1910	Homewood CC, Flossmoor, Ill.		Dorothy I. Campbell	Mrs G. M. Martin	2 & 1
1911	Baltusrol HC, Springfield, NJ		Margaret Curtis	Lillian B. Hyde	5 & 3
1912	Essex CC, Manchester, Mass.		Margaret Curtis	Mrs R. H. Barlow	3 & 2
1913	Wilmington CC, Wilmington, Del.		Gladys Ravenscroft	Marion Hollins	2 up
1914	Nassau CC, Glen Cove, NY		Mrs H. Arnold Jackson	Elaine V. Rosenthal	1 up
1915	Onwentsia Club, Lake Forest, Ill.		Mrs C. H. Vanderbeck	Mrs W. A. Gavin	3 & 2
1916	Belmont Springs CC, Waverly, Mass.		Alexa Stirling	Mildred Caverly	2 & 1
1917–18	Not played				
1919	Shawnee CC, Shawnee-on-Delaware, Pa		Alexa Stirling	Mrs. W. A. Gavin	6 & 5
1920	Mayfield CC, Cleveland, Ohio		Alexa Stirling	Mrs J. V. Hurd	5 & 4
1921	Hollywood GC, Deal, NJ		Marion Hollins	Alexa Stirling	5 & 4
1922	Greenbrier GC, White Sulphur Springs, WV		Glenna Collett	Mrs W. A. Gavin	5 & 4
1923	Westchester-Biltmore CC, Rye, NY		Edith Cummings	Alexa Stirling	3 & 2
1924	Rhode Island CC, Nayatt, RI		Mrs J. V. Hurd	Mary K. Browne	7 & 6
1925	St Louis CC, Clayton, Mo.		Glenna Collett	Mrs W. G. Fraser	9 & 8
1926	Merion Cricket Club, Haverford, Pa		Mrs G. Henry Stetson	Mrs W. D. Goss, Jr	3 & 1
1927	Cherry Valley Club, Garden City, NY		Mrs M. B. Horn	Maureen Orcutt	5 & 4
1928	Virginia Hot Springs G & TC, Hot Springs, Va		Glenna Collett	Virginia Van Wie	13 & 12
1929	Oakland Hills CC, Birmingham, Mich.		Glenna Collett	Leona Pressler	4 & 3
1930	Los Angeles CC, Beverly Hills, Calif.		Glenna Collett	Virginia Van Wie	6 & 5
1931	CC of Buffalo, Williamsville, NY		Helen Hicks	Mrs E. H. Vare, Jr	2 & 1
1932	Salem CC, Peabody, Mass.		Virginia Van Wie	Mrs E. H. Vare, Jr	10 & 8
1933	Exmoor CC, Highland Park, Ill.		Virginia Van Wie	Helen Hicks	4 & 3
1934	Whitemarsh Valley CC, Chestnut Hill, Pa		Virginia Van Wie	Dorothy Traung	2 & 1
1935	Interlochen CC, Hopkins, Minn.		Mrs E. H. Vare, Jr	Patty Berg	3 & 2
1936	Canoe Brook CC, Summit, NJ		Pamela Barton	Mrs J. D. Crews	4 & 3
1937	Memphis CC, Memphis, Tenn.		Mrs J. A. Page, Jr	Patty Berg	7 & 6
1938	Westmoreland CC, Wilmette, Ill.		Patty Berg	Mrs J. A. Page, Jr	6 & 5
1939	Wee Burn Club, Noroton, Conn.		Betty Jameson	Dorothy Kirby	3 & 2
1940	Del Monte G & CC, Del Monte, Calif.		Betty Jameson	Jane S. Cothran	6 & 5
1941	The Country Club, Brookline, Mass.		Mrs F. Newell	Helen Sigel	5 & 3
1942–45	Not played				
1946	Southern Hills CC, Tulsa, Okla		Mrs G. Zaharias	Clara C. Sherman	11 & 9
1947	Franklin Hills CC, Franklin, Mich.		Louise Suggs	Dorothy Kirby	2 up
1948	Del Monte G & TC, Del Monte, Calif.		Mrs G. S. Lenczyk	Helen Sigel	4 & 3
1949	Merion GC, Ardmore, Pa		Mrs M. A Porter	Dorothy Kielty	3 & 2
1950	Atlanta AC (East Lake), Atlanta, Ga		Beverly Hanson	Mae Murray	6 & 4
1951	Town & CC, St Paul, Minn.		Dorothy Kirby	Claire Doran	2 & 1
1952	Waverley CC, Portland, Ore.		Jacqueline Pung	Shirley McFedters	2 & 1
1953	Rhode Island CC, West Barrington, RI		Mary Lena Faulk	Polly Riley	3 & 2
1954	Allegheny CC, Sewickley, Pa		Barbara Romack	Mary K. Wright	4 & 2
1955	Myers Park CC, Charlotte, NC		Patricia A. Lesser	Jane Nelson	7 & 6
1956	Meridian Hills CC, Indianapolis, Ind.		Marlene Stewart	Jo Anne Gunderson	2 & 1
1957	Del Paso CC, Sacramento, Calif.		Jo Anne Gunderson	Mrs Les Johnstone	8 & 6
1958	Wee Burn CC, Darien, Conn.		Anne Quast	Barbara Romack	3 & 2
1959	Congressional CC, Washington, DC		Barbara McIntire	Jo Anne Goodwin	4 & 3
1960	Tulsa CC, Tulsa, Okla		Jo Anne Gunderson	Jean Ashley	6 & 5
1961	Tacoma C & GC, Tacoma, Wash.		Mrs J. D. Decker	Phyllis Preuss	14 & 13
1962	CC of Rochester, Rochester, NY		Jo Anne Gunderson	Ann Baker	9 & 8
1963	Taconic GC, Williamstown, Mass.		Mrs J. D. Welts	Peggy Conley	2 & 1
1964	Prairie Dunes CC, Hutchinson, Kans.		Barbara McIntire	Jo Anne Gunderson	3 & 2
1965	Lakewood CC, Denver, Colo		Jean Ashley	Mrs D. Welts	5 & 4
1966	Sewickly Heights GC, Sewickly, Pa		Mrs D. R. Carner	Mrs J. D. Streit	41 holes
1967	Annandale GC, Pasadena, Calif.		Mary Lou Dill	Jean Ashley	5 & 4
1968	Birmingham CC, Mich.		Mrs D. R. Carner	Mrs D Welts	5 & 4
1969	Las Colinas CC, Irving, Texas		Catherine Lacoste	Shelley Hamlin	3 & 2
1970	Wee Burn CC, Darien, Conn.		Martha Wilkinson	Cynthia Hill	3 & 2
1971	Atlanta CC, Atlanta, Ga		Laura Baugh	Beth Barry	1 up
1972	St Louis CC, St Louis, Mo.		Mary Budke	Cynthia Hill	5 & 4
1973	Montclair CC, NJ		Carol Semple	Mrs Anne Sander	1 up
1974	Broadmoor CC, Seattle, Wash.		Cynthia Hill	Carol Semple	5 & 4

British Ladies Amateur Championship

A match-play tournament, first played in 1893 at Lytham St Anne's, Lancashire, it has grown to become the major European women's event.

Year	Winner
1893	Lady Margaret Scott
1894	Lady Margaret Scott
1895	Lady Margaret Scott
1896	A. B. Pascoe
1897	E. C. Orr
1898	L. Thomson
1899	May Hezlet
1900	Rhona K. Adair
1901	Molly A. Graham
1902	May Hezlet
1903	Rhona K. Adair
1904	Lottie Dod
1905	B. Thompson
1906	Mrs W. Kennion
1907	May Hezlet
1908	M. Titterton
1909	Dorothy Campbell
1910	G. Suttie
1911	Dorothy Campbell
1912	Gladys Ravencroft
1913	Muriel Dodd
1914	Cecil Leitch
1915–19	Not played
1920	Cecil Leitch
1921	Cecil Leitch
1922	Joyce Wethered
1923	Doris Chambers
1924	Joyce Wethered
1925	Joyce Wethered
1926	Cecil Leitch
1927	Simone Thion de la Chaume
1928	Nanette LeBlan
1929	Joyce Wethered
1930	Diana Fishwick
1931	Enid Wilson
1932	Enid Wilson
1933	Enid Wilson
1934	Mrs A. M. Holm
1935	Wanda Morgan
1936	Pamela Barton
1937	Jessie Anderson
1938	Mrs A. M. Holm
1939	Pamela Barton
1940–45	Not played
1946	Mrs G. W. Hetherington
1947	Mrs George Zaharias
1948	Louise Suggs
1949	Frances Stephens
1950	Vicomtesse de Saint Sauveur
1951	Mrs P. G. Maccann
1952	Moira Paterson
1953	Marlene Stewart
1954	Frances Stephens
1955	Mrs G. Valentine
1956	Wiffi Smith
1957	Philomena Garvey
1958	Mrs G. Valentine
1959	Elizabeth Price
1960	Barbara McIntire
1961	Mrs A. D. Spearman
1962	Mrs A. D. Spearman
1963	Brigitte Varangot
1964	Carol Sorenson
1965	Brigitte Varangot
1966	E. Chadwick
1967	E. Chadwick
1968	Brigitte Varangot
1969	Catherine Lacoste
1970	Dinah Oxley
1971	Michelle Walker
1972	Michelle Walker
1973	A. Irvin
1974	C. Semple

LPGA Championship (USA)

Organized by the women's equivalent of the PGA, this championship is played over 54 holes stroke play.

Year	Winner	Runner-Up	Score
1955	Beverly Hanson	Louise Suggs	220 −4 & 3
1956	Marlene Hagge	Patty Berg	291
1957	Louise Suggs	Wiffi Smith	285
1958	Mickey Wright	Fay Crocker	288
1959	Betsy Rawls	Patty Berg	288
1960	Mickey Wright	Louise Suggs	292
1961	Mickey Wright	Louise Suggs	287
1962	Judy Kimball	Shirley Spork	282
1963	Mickey Wright	Mary Lena Faulk, Mary Mills Louise Suggs	294
1964	Mary Mills	Mickey Wright	278
1965	Sandra Haynie	Clifford Ann Creed	279
1966	Gloria Ehret	Mickey Wright	282
1967	Kathy Whitworth	Shirley Englehorn	284
1968	Sandra Post	Kathy Whitworth	294
1969	Betsy Rawls	Susie Berning, Carol Mann	293
1970	Shirley Englehorn	Kathy Whitworth	285
1971	Kathy Whitworth	Kathy Ahern	288
1972	Kathy Ahern	J. Blalock	293
1973	Mary Mills	B. Burfeindt	288
1974	Sandra Haynie	J. Garner	288

United States Women's Open Championship

First sponsored by the Women's Professional Golfers' Association, 1946, and subsequently by the Ladies' PGA (1949–52) and the USGA (from 1953), this is a 72-hole stroke play event.

Year	Site	Winner	Runner-Up	Score
1946	Spokane CC, Spokane, Wash.	Patty Berg	Betty Jameson	5 & 4
1947	Starmount CC, Greensboro, NC	Betty Jameson	Sally Sessions, Polly Riley	295
1948	Atlantic City CC, Northfield, NJ	Mrs George Zaharias	Betty Hicks	300
1949	Prince Georges G & CC, Landover, Md	Louise Suggs	Mrs George Zaharias	291
1950	Rolling Hills CC, Wichita, Kans.	Mrs George Zaharias	Betsy Rawls	291
1951	Druid Hills GC, Atlanta, Ga	Betsy Rawls	Louise Suggs	293
1952	Bala GC, Philadelphia, Pa	Louise Suggs	Marlene Bauer, Betty Jameson	284
1953	CC of Rochester, Rochester, NY	Betsy Rawls	Mrs Jacqueline Pung	302
1954	Salem CC, Peabody, Mass.	Mrs George Zaharias	Betty Hicks	291
1955	Wichita CC, Wichita, Kans.	Fay Crocker	Louise Suggs, Mary L. Faulk	299
1956	Northland CC, Duluth, Minn.	Kathy Cornelius	Barbara McIntire	302
1957	Winged Foot GC, Mamaroneck, NY	Betsy Rawls	Patty Berg	299
1958	Forest Lake CC, Bloomfield Hills, Mich.	M. K. (Mickey) Wright	Louise Suggs	290
1959	Churchill Valley CC, Pittsburgh, Pa	M. K. (Mickey) Wright	Louise Suggs	287
1960	Worcester CC, Worcester, Mass.	Betsy Rawls	Joyce Ziske	292
1961	Baltusrol GC, Springfield, NJ	M. K. (Mickey) Wright	Betsy Rawls	293
1962	Dunes G & BC, Myrtle Beach, SC	Mrs Murie Mackenzie Lindstrom	Ruth Jessen, Jo Anne Prentice	301
1963	Kenwood CC, Cincinnati, Ohio	Mary Mills	Sandra Haynie, Louise Suggs	289
1964	San Diego CC, Chula Vista, Calif.	M. K. (Mickey) Wright	Ruth Jessen	290
1965	Atlantic City CC, Northfield, NJ	Carol Mann	Kathy Cornelius	290
1966	Hazeltine Nat. GC, Minneapolis, Minn.	Sandra Spuzich	Carol Mann	297
1967	Virginia Hot Springs G & TC, Hot Springs, Va	Catherine Lacoste	Susie Maxwell, Beth Stone	294
1968	Moselem Springs GC, Fleetwood, Pa	Mrs Susie Berning	M. K. (Mickey) Wright	289
1969	Scenic Hills CC, Pensacola, Fla	Donna Caponi	Peggy Wilson	294
1970	Muskogee CC, Muskogee, Okla	Donna Caponi	Sandra Haynie, Sandra Spuzich	287
1971	Kahkwa CC, Erie, Pa	Mrs JoAnne Gunderson Carner	Kathy Whitworth	288
1972	Winged Foot GC, Mamaroneck, NY	Mrs Susie Berning	Pam Barnett, Kathy Ahern, Judy Rankin	299
1973	CC of Rochester, Rochester, NY	Mrs Susie Berning		290
1974	La Grange CC, Ill.	Miss Sandra Haynie		295

World Seniors Championship

Year	Site	Winner	Runner-Up	Score
1961	Fairhaven, UK	P. Runyan	S. L. King	3 & 1
1962	Prestwick, UK	P. Runyan	S. L. King	2 & 1
1963	St Annes, UK	H. Barron	G. Evans	3 & 2
1964	Wentworth, UK	S. Snead	S. S. Scott	7 & 6
1965	Formby, UK	S. Snead	C. H. Ward	1 up (37 holes)
1966	Dalmahoy, UK	F. Haas	D. Rees	3 & 2
1967	Wallasey, UK	J. Panton	S. Snead	3 & 2
1968	Downfield, UK	C. Harper	M. Faulkner	2 up
1969	Portsmouth, USA	T. Bolt	J. Panton	1 up (39 holes)
1970	Portsmouth, USA	S. Snead	M. Faulkner	3 & 2
1971	Portsmouth, USA	K. Nagle	J. Boros	4 & 3
1972	Longniddry, UK	S. Snead	K. Bousfield	3 & 2
1973	Portsmouth, USA	S. Snead	K. Nagle	1 up (41 holes)
1974	Lundin, UK	R. DeVicenzo	E. Lester	5 & 4

Walker Cup Match

Biennial amateur men's team match between the United States and the United Kingdom (including the Republic of Ireland), named after George H. Walker, President of the USGA. The matches take place alternately in the United States and the United Kingdom, and now consist of four 18-hole foursomes and eight 18-hole singles (match play) on each of two days.

Year	Site	Winner	Loser	Score
1922	National Golf Links of America, Southampton, NY	United States	British Isles	8 to 4
1923	St Andrews, Scotland	United States	British Isles	6 to 5, one match halved
1924	Garden City Golf Club, Garden City, NY	United States	British Isles	9 to 3
1926	St Andrews, Scotland	United States	British Isles	6 to 5, one match halved
1928	Chicago Golf Club, Wheaton, Ill.	United States	British Isles	11 to 1
1930	Royal St George's GC, Sandwich, England	United States	British Isles	10 to 2
1932	The Country Club, Brookline, Mass.	United States	British Isles	8 to 1, three matches halved
1934	St Andrews, Scotland	United States	British Isles	9 to 2, one match halved
1936	Pine Valley Golf Club, Clementon, NJ	United States	British Isles	9 to 0, three matches halved
1938	St Andrews, Scotland	British Isles	United States	7 to 4, one match halved
1947	St Andrews, Scotland	United States	British Isles	8 to 4
1949	Winged Foot GC, Mamaroneck, NY	United States	British Isles	10 to 2
1951	Royal Birkdale Golf Club, Southport, England	United States	British Isles	6 to 3, three matches halved
1953	Kittansett Club, Marion, Mass.	United States	British Isles	9 to 3
1955	St Andrews, Scotland	United States	British Isles	10 to 2
1957	Minikahda Club, Minneapolis, Minn.	United States	British Isles	8 to 3, one match halved
1959	Honourable Company of Edinburgh Golfers, Muirfield, Scotland	United States	British Isles	9 to 3
1961	Seattle Golf Club, Seattle, Wash.	United States	British Isles	11 to 1
1963	Ailsa Course, Turnberry, Scotland	United States	British Isles	12 to 8, four matches halved
1965	Baltimore CC, Five Farms, Baltimore, Md	Tie		11 to 11, two matches halved
1967	Royal St George's GC, Sandwich, England	United States	British Isles	13 to 7, four matches halved
1969	Milwaukee CC, Milwaukee, Wis.	United States	British Isles	10 to 8, six matches halved
1971	St Andrews, Scotland	British Isles	United States	12 to 10, two matches halved
1973	The Country Club, Brookline, Mass.	United States	British Isles	12 to 8, four matches halved

Curtis Cup Match

Biennial amateur women's team match between the United States and the United Kingdom (including the Republic of Ireland). Since 1964 the teams have played three 18-hole foursomes and six 18-hole singles (match play) on each of two days. The matches take place alternately in the United States and the United Kingdom. The Cup was presented by the sisters Harriot and Margaret Curtis.

Year	Site	Winner	Loser	Score
1932	Wentworth Golf Club, Wentworth, England	United States	British Isles	5½ to 3½
1934	Chevy Chase Club, Chevy Chase, Md.	United States	British Isles	6½ to 2½
1936	King's Course, Gleneagles, Scotland	United States	British Isles	4½ to 4½
1938	Essex Country Club, Manchester, Mass.	United States	British Isles	5½ to 3½
1948	Royal Birkdale Golf Club, Southport, England	United States	British Isles	6½ to 2½
1950	CC of Buffalo, Williamsville, NY	United States	British Isles	7½ to 1½
1952	Honourable Company of Edinburgh Golfers, Muirfield, Scotland	British Isles	United States	5 to 4

1954	Merion GC (East Course), Ardmore, Pa	United States	British Isles	6 to 3
1956	Prince's GC, Sandwich Bay, England	British Isles	United States	5 to 4
1958	Brae Burn CC, West Newton, Mass.	British Isles	United States	$4\frac{1}{2}$ to $4\frac{1}{2}$
1960	Lindrick GC, Worksop, England	United States	British Isles	$6\frac{1}{2}$ to $2\frac{1}{2}$
1962	Broadmoor GC (East Course), Colorado Springs, Colo	United States	British Isles	8 to 1
1964	Royal Porthcawl GC, Porthcawl, South Wales	United States	British Isles	$10\frac{1}{2}$ to $7\frac{1}{2}$
1966	Virginia Hot Springs Golf & Tennis Club (Cascades Course), Hot Springs, Va	United States	British Isles	13 to 5
1968	Royal County Downs GC, Newcastle, Northern Ireland	United States	British Isles	$10\frac{1}{2}$ to $7\frac{1}{2}$
1970	Brae Burn CC, West Newton, Mass.	United States	British Isles	$11\frac{1}{2}$ to $6\frac{1}{2}$
1972	Western Gailes GC, Scotland	United States	British Isles	10 to 8
1974	San Francisco	United States	British Isles	13 to 5

Ryder Cup Match

Biennial match (match play) played between representatives of the United States and British PGAs, alternating between the two countries. The format has varied considerably over the years. In the last Ryder Cup (1973), four 18-hole foursomes were played in the mornings of the first two days, with four four-balls in the afternoons. On the third and final day eight 18-hole singles were played both in the morning and the afternoon. The solid gold trophy was presented by Samuel A. Ryder, a British seed merchant.

Year	Site	Winner	Loser	Score
1927	Worcester CC, Worcester, Mass.	United States	British Isles	$9\frac{1}{2}$ to $2\frac{1}{2}$
1929	Moortown, England	British Isles	United States	7 to 5
1931	Scioto CC, Columbus, Ohio	United States	British Isles	9 to 3
1933	Royal Birkdale GC, Southport, England	British Isles	United States	$6\frac{1}{2}$ to $5\frac{1}{2}$
1935	Ridgewood CC, Ridgewood, NJ	United States	British Isles	9 to 3
1937	Royal Birkdale GC, Southport, England	United States	British Isles	8 to 4
1947	Portland GC, Portland, Ore.	United States	British Isles	11 to 1
1949	Ganton GC, Scarborough, England	United States	British Isles	7 to 5
1951	Pinehurst CC, Pinehurst, NC	United States	British Isles	$9\frac{1}{2}$ to $2\frac{1}{2}$
1953	Wentworth Club, England	United States	British Isles	$6\frac{1}{2}$ to $5\frac{1}{2}$
1955	Thunderbird Ranch & CC, Palm Springs, Calif.	United States	British Isles	8 to 4
1957	Lindrick GC, Yorkshire, England	British Isles	United States	$7\frac{1}{2}$ to $4\frac{1}{2}$
1959	Eldorado CC, Palm Desert, Calif.	United States	British Isles	$8\frac{1}{2}$ to $3\frac{1}{2}$
1961	Royal Lytham & St Anne's GC, St Anne's-on-the-Sea, England	United States	British Isles	$14\frac{1}{2}$ to $9\frac{1}{2}$
1963	East Lake CC, Atlanta, Ga	United States	British Isles	23 to 9
1965	Royal Birkdale GC, Southport, England	United States	British Isles	$19\frac{1}{2}$ to $12\frac{1}{2}$
1967	Champion GC, Houston, Texas	United States	British Isles	$23\frac{1}{2}$ to $8\frac{1}{2}$
1969	Royal Birkdale GC, Southport, England	United States	British Isles	16 to 16
1971	Old Warson CC, St Louis, Mo.	United States	British Isles	$18\frac{1}{2}$ to $13\frac{1}{2}$
1973	Muirfield GC, Scotland	United States	British Isles	19 to 13

World Cup Match

Called the Canada Cup until 1967, this contest was inaugurated by a Canadian industrialist, John Jay Hopkins. It is an international event, competed for by two-man teams from over forty countries. It is played over 72 holes (stroke play).

Year	Site	Winner	Runner-Up	Score
1953	Beaconsfield GC, Montreal	**Argentina** Antonio Cerda, Roberto DeVicenzo	**Canada** Stan Leonard, Bill Kerr	287
1954	Laval-sur-le-Lac, Montreal	**Australia** Peter W. Thomson, K. D. G. Nagle	**Argentina** Antonio Cerda, Roberto DeVicenzo	556
1955	Columbia CC, Washington, DC	**United States** Ed Furgol, Chick Harbert	**Australia** Peter W. Thomson, K. D. G. Nagle	560
1956	Wentworth Club, England	**United States** Ben Hogan, Sam Snead	**South Africa** A. D. Locke, Gary Player	567
1957	Kasumigaseki GC, Tokyo	**Japan** Torakichi Nakamura, Koichi Ono	**United States** Sam Snead, Jimmy Demaret	557
1958	Mexico GC, Mexico City	**Ireland** Harry Bradshaw, Christy O'Connor	**Spain** Angel Miguel, Sebastian Miguel	579
1959	Royal Melbourne GC, Melbourne	**Australia** Peter W. Thomson, K. D. G. Nagle	**United States** Sam Snead, Cary Middlecoff	563
1960	Portmarnock GC, Dublin	**United States** Sam Snead, Arnold Palmer	**England** Harry Weetman, Bernard Hunt	565
1961	Dorado GC, Puerto Rico	**United States** Sam Snead, Jimmy Demaret	**Australia** Peter W. Thomson, K. D. G. Nagle	560
1962	Jockey Golf Club of San Isidro, Buenos Aires	**United States** Arnold Palmer, Sam Snead	**Argentina** Roberto DeVicenzo, Fidel DeLuca	557
1963	Saint Nom la Breteche Club, Versailles	**United States** Jack Nicklaus, Arnold Palmer	**Spain** Sebastian Miguel, Ramon Sota	482
1964	Royal Kaanapali Golf Course, Maui, Hawaii	**United States** Jack Nicklaus, Arnold Palmer	**Argentina** Roberto DeVicenzo, L. Ruiz	554
1965	Club de Campo, Madrid	**South Africa** Gary Player, Harold R. Henning	**Spain** Angel Miguel, Ramon Sota	571
1966	Yomiuri CC, Tokyo	**United States** Arnold Palmer, Jack Nicklaus	**South Africa** Gary Player, Harold R. Henning	548
1967	Club de Golf Mexico, Mexico City	**United States** Arnold Palmer, Jack Nicklaus	**New Zealand** Robert J. Charles, Walter Godfrey	557
1968	Circolo Golf Olgiata, Rome	**Canada** Al Balding, George Knudson	**United States** Julius Boros, Lee Trevino	569
1969	Singapore Island CC, Singapore	**United States** Orville Moody, Lee Trevino	**Japan** T. Kono, H. Yasuda	552
1970	Jockey Golf Club of San Isidro, Buenos Aires	**Australia** David Graham, Bruce Devlin	**Argentina** Roberto DeVicenzo, V. Fernàndez	545
1971	PGA National GC, Palm Beach Gardens	**United States** Jack Nicklaus, Lee Trevino	**South Africa** Gary Player, Harold R. Henning	555
1972	Royal Melbourne GC, Melbourne	**Taiwan** Hsieh Min-nan, Liang Huan-Lu	**Japan** Takaaki Kono, Takashi Murakami	438
1973	Nueva Andalucia GC, Spain	**United States** Jack Nicklaus, Johnny Miller	**South Africa** Gary Player, Hugh Baiocchi	558
1974	Caracas, Venezuela	**South Africa** Bobby Cole, Dale Hayes	**Japan** I. Aoki, M. Ozaki	554

International Trophy
Awarded to the lowest scoring player in the World Cup Match. Though it was not awarded in the first year of the World Cup (Canada Cup), Antonio Cerda would have been the winner.

Year	Winner	Score
1954	Stan Leonard, Canada	275
1955	Ed Furgol, United States	279
1956	Ben Hogan, United States	277
1957	Torakichi Nakamura, Japan	274
1958	Angel Miguel, Spain	286
1959	Stan Leonard, Canada	275
1960	Flory Van Donck, Belgium	279
1961	Sam Snead, United States	272
1962	Roberto DeVicenzo, Argentina	276
1963	Jack Nicklaus, United States	237
1964	Jack Nicklaus, United States	276
1965	Gary Player, South Africa	281
1966	George Knudson, Canada	272
1967	Arnold Palmer, United States	276
1968	Al Balding, Canada	274
1969	Lee Trevino, United States	275
1970	Roberto DeVicenzo, Argentina	269
1971	Jack Nicklaus, United States	271
1972	Hsieh Min-nàn, Taiwan	217
1973	Johnny Miller, United States	277
1974	Bobby Cole, South Africa	271

Open Championships
There follows a list of the winners of some of the more important Open Championships.

Argentine Open

Year	Winner
1905	Mungo Park
1906	J. C. Avery Wright
1907	Mungo Park
1908	F. A. Sutton
1909	Raul Castillo
1910	A. Philp
1911	Rudolfo Castillo
1912	Mungo Park
1913	A. Philp
1914	Raul Castillo
1915	L. Gonzalez
1916	L. Gonzalez
1917	L. Gonzalez
1918	J. A. Eustace
1919	Raul Castillo
1920	J. Jurado
1921	A. Perez
1922	A. Perez
1923	A. Perez
1924	J. Jurado
1925	J. Jurado
1926	M. Churio
1927	J. Jurado
1928	J. Jurado
1929	J. Jurado
1930	T. Genta
1931	J. Jurado
1932	A. Perez
1933	M. Pose
1934	M. Churio
1935	J. I. Cruickshank
1936	J. I. Cruickshank
1937	Henry Picard
1938	Paul Runyan
1939	M. Pose
1940	Mario Gonzalez
1941	Jimmy Demaret
1942	M. Martin
1943	M. Churio
1944	R. DeVicenzo
1945	Not played
1946	Lloyd Mangrum
1947	E. Bertolino
1948	A. Cerda
1949	R. DeVicenzo
1950	M. Pose
1951	R. DeVicenzo
1952	R. DeVicenzo
1953	Mario Gonzalez
1954	F. DeLuca
1955	E. Bertolino
1956	A. Cerda
1957	L. Ruiz
1958	R. DeVicenzo
1959	L. Ruiz
1960	F. DeLuca
1961	F. DeLuca
1962	A. Miguel
1963	J. Ledesma
1964	E. Nari
1965	R. DeVicenzo
1966	J. Castillo
1967	R. DeVicenzo
1968	V. Fernandez
1969	V. Fernandez
1970	R. DeVicenzo
1971	F. Molina
1972	R. DeVicenzo

Australian Open

Year	Winner
1904	Michael Scott
1905	D. Soutar
1906	Carnegie Clark
1907	Michael Scott
1908	Clyde Pearce
1909	C. Felstead
1910	Carnegie Clark
1911	Carnegie Clark
1912	Ivo Whitton
1913	Ivo Whitton
1914–19	Not played
1920	J. H. Kirkwood
1921	A. LeFavre
1922	C. Campbell
1923	T. E. Howard
1924	A. Russell
1925	F. Popplewell
1926	Ivo Whitton
1927	R. Stewart
1928	F. Popplewell
1929	Ivo Whitton
1930	F. P. Eyre
1931	Ivo Whitton
1932	M. J. Ryan
1933	M. L. Kelly
1934	W. J. Bolger
1935	F. McMahon
1936	Gene Sarazen
1937	G. Naismith
1938	Jim Ferrier
1939	Jim Ferrier
1940–45	Not played
1946	H. O. Pickworth
1947	H. O. Pickworth
1948	H. O. Pickworth
1949	E. Cremin
1950	N. G. Von Nida
1951	Peter W. Thomson
1952	N. G. Von Nida
1953	N. G. Von Nida
1954	H. O. Pickworth
1955	A. D. Locke
1956	Bruce Crampton
1957	F. Phillips
1958	Gary Player
1959	K. D. G. Nagle
1960	Bruce Devlin
1961	F. Phillips
1962	Gary Player
1963	Gary Player

1964	Jack Nicklaus
1965	Gary Player
1966	Arnold Palmer
1967	Peter W. Thomson
1968	Jack Nicklaus
1969	Gary Player
1970	Gary Player
1971	Jack Nicklaus
1972	Peter W. Thomson
1973	J. C. Snead
1974	Gary Player

Brazilian Open

Year	Winner
1945	M. Pose
1946	Mario Gonzalez
1947	Not played
1948	Mario Gonzalez
1949	Mario Gonzalez
1950	Mario Gonzalez
1951	Mario Gonzalez
1952	Sam Snead
1953	Mario Gonzalez
1954	R. DeVicenzo
1955	Mario Gonzalez
1956	F. DeLuca
1957	R. DeVicenzo
1958	Billy Casper, Jr
1959	Billy Casper, Jr
1960	R. DeVicenzo
1961	P. Alliss
1962	B. J. Hunt
1963	R. DeVicenzo
1964	R. DeVicenzo
1965	Not played
1966	Rex Baxter
1967	Not played
1968	T. Kono
1969	Manuel Gonzalez
1970	Bert Greene
1971	Bruce Fleisher
1972	Gary Player

Canadian Open

Year	Winner
1904	J. H. Oke
1905	George Cumming
1906	C. R. Murray
1907	Percy Barrett
1908	Albert Murray
1909	Karl Keffer
1910	D. Kenny
1911	C. R. Murray
1912	George Sargent
1913	Albert Murray
1914	Karl Keffer
1915–18	Not played
1919	J. Douglas Edgar
1920	J. Douglas Edgar
1921	William Trovinger
1922	Al Watrous
1923	Clarence Hackney
1924	Leo Diegel
1925	Leo Diegel

1926	Macdonald Smith
1927	Tommy Armour
1928	Leo Diegel
1929	Leo Diegel
1930	Tommy Armour
1931	Walter Hagen
1932	Harry Cooper
1933	Joe Kirkwood
1934	Tommy Armour
1935	G. Kunes
1936	W. Lawson Little
1937	Harry Cooper
1938	Sam Snead
1939	Harold McSpaden
1940	Sam Snead
1941	Sam Snead
1942	Craig Wood
1943–44	Not played
1945	Byron Nelson
1946	George Fazio
1947	A. D. Locke
1948	C. Congdon
1949	E. J. Harrison
1950	Jim Ferrier
1951	Jim Ferrier
1952	John Palmer
1953	Dave Douglas
1954	Pat Fletcher
1955	Arnold Palmer
1956	Doug Sanders
1957	George Bayer
1958	Wes Ellis, Jr
1959	Doug Ford
1960	Art Wall, Jr
1961	Jack Cupit
1962	Ted Kroll
1963	Doug Ford
1964	K. D. G. Nagle
1965	Gene Littler
1966	Don Massengale
1967	Billy Casper, Jr
1968	R. J. Charles
1969	Tommy Aaron
1970	Kermit Zarley
1971	Lee Trevino
1972	Gay Brewer
1973	Tom Weiskopf
1974	R. Nichols

Dutch Open

Year	Winner
1919	D. Oosterveer
1920	H. Burrows
1921	H. Burrows
1922	Geo. Pannell
1923	H. Burrows
1924	Aubrey Boomer
1925	Aubrey Boomer
1926	Aubrey Boomer
1927	Percy Boomer
1928	E. R. Whitcombe
1929	J. J. Taylor
1930	J. Oosterveer
1931	F. Dyer

1932	A. Boyer
1933	M. Dallemagne
1934	S. F. Brews
1935	S. F. Brews
1936	F. Van Donck
1937	F. Van Donck
1938	A. H. Padgham
1939	A. D. Locke
1940–47	Not played
1948	Cecil Denny
1949	J. Adams
1950	R. DeVicenzo
1951	F. Van Donck
1952	Cecil Denny
1953	F. Van Donck
1954	Ugo Grappasonni
1955	A. Angelini
1956	A. Cerda
1957	J. Jacobs
1958	D. Thomas
1959	S. Sewgolum
1960	S. Sewgolum
1961	B. B. S. Wilkes
1962	B. G. C. Huggett
1963	R. Waltman
1964	S. Sewgolum
1965	A. Miguel
1966	R. Sota
1967	P. Townsend
1968	J. Cockin
1969	Guy Wolstenholme
1970	Vicente Fernandez
1971	Ramon Sota
1972	Jack Newton
1973	D. McClelland
1974	Brian Barnes

French Open

Year	Winner
1906	A. Massy
1907	A. Massy
1908	J. H. Taylor
1909	J. H. Taylor
1910	James Braid
1911	A. Massy
1912	Jean Gassiat
1913	George Duncan
1914	J. Douglas Edgar
1915–19	Not played
1920	Walter Hagen
1921	Aubrey Boomer
1922	Aubrey Boomer
1923	Jas. Ockenden
1924	C. J. H. Tolley
1925	A. Massy
1926	Aubrey Boomer
1927	George Duncan
1928	C. J. H. Tolley
1929	Aubrey Boomer
1930	E. R. Whitcombe
1931	Aubrey Boomer
1932	A. J. Lacey
1933	B. Gadd
1934	S. F. Brews

1935	S. F. Brews
1936	M. Dallemagne
1937	M. Dallemagne
1938	M. Dallemagne
1939	M. Pose
1940–45	Not played
1946	T. Henry Cotton
1947	T. Henry Cotton
1948	F. Cavalo
1949	U. Grappasonni
1950	R. DeVicenzo
1951	H. Hassanein
1952	A. D. Locke
1953	A. D. Locke
1954	F. Van Donck
1955	Byron Nelson
1956	A. Miguel
1957	F. Van Donck
1958	F. Van Donck
1959	D. C. Thomas
1960	R. DeVicenzo
1961	K. D. G. Nagle
1962	A. Murray
1963	B. Devlin
1964	R. DeVicenzo
1965	R. Sota
1966	D. J. Hutchinson
1967	B. J. Hunt
1968	P. J. Butler
1969	J. Garaialde
1970	David Graham
1971	Liang Huan-Lu
1972	Barry Jaeckel
1973	P. Oosterhuis
1974	P. Oosterhuis

German Open

Year	Winner
1911	Harry Vardon
1912	John H. Taylor
1913–25	Not played
1926	P. Alliss
1927	P. Alliss
1928	P. Alliss
1929	P. Alliss
1930	A. Boyer
1931	R. Golias
1932	A. Boyer
1933	P. Alliss
1934	A. H. Padgham
1935	A. Boyer
1936	A. Boyer
1937	T. Henry Cotton
1938	T. Henry Cotton
1939	T. Henry Cotton
1940–50	Not played
1951	A. Cerda
1952	A. Cerda
1953	F. Van Donck
1954	A. D. Locke
1955	K. Bousfield
1956	F. Van Donck
1957	H. Weetman
1958	F. DeLuca

1959	K. Bousfield
1960	Peter W. Thomson
1961	B. J. Hunt
1962	F. R. Verwey
1963	B. G. C. Huggett
1964	R. DeVicenzo
1965	H. R. Henning
1966	R. Stanton
1967	D. Swaelens
1968	B. Franklin
1969	J. Garaialde
1970	J. Garaialde
1971	Neil Coles
1972	Graham Marsh
1973	F. Abreu
1974	S. Owen

Hong Kong Open

Year	Winner
1959	Liang Huan-Lu
1960	Peter W. Thomson
1961	K. D. G. Nagle
1962	Len Woodward
1963	Hsieh Yung Yo
1964	Hsieh Yung Yo
1965	Peter W. Thomson
1966	F. Phillips
1967	Peter W. Thomson
1968	R. Vines
1969	Teruo Sugihara
1970	Isao Katsumata
1971	Orville Moody
1972	Walter Godfrey
1973	F. Phillips
1974	Liang Huan-Lu

Indian Open

Year	Winner
1963	Peter W. Thomson
1965	P. G. Sethi
1966	Peter W. Thomson
1967	K. Hosoishi
1968	K. Hosoishi
1969	B. Arda
1970	Chen Chien Chin
1971	Graham Marsh
1972	Bryan Jones
1973	Graham Marsh
1974	Chie-Hsiung Kuo

Italian Open

Year	Winner
1925	F. Pasquali
1926	A. Boyer
1927	Percy Alliss
1928	A. Boyer
1929	R. Gollas
1930	A. Boyer
1931	A. Boyer
1932	A. Boomer
1933	Not played
1934	N. Nutley
1935	Percy Alliss
1936	T. H. Cotton

1937	M. Dallemagne
1938	F. Van Donck
1939–46	Not played
1947	F. Van Donck
1948	A. Casera
1949	H. Hassanein
1950	U. Grappasonni
1951	J. Adams
1952	E. C. Brown
1953	F. Van Donck
1954	U. Grappasonni
1955	F. Van Donck
1956	A. Cerda
1957	H. R. Henning
1958	Peter Alliss
1959	Peter W. Thomson
1960	B. B. S. Wilkes
1961–70	Not played
1971	R. Sota
1972	N. Wood
1973	A. Jacklin
1974	P. Oosterhuis

Japanese Open

Year	Winner
1927	R. Akahoshi
1928	R. Asami
1929	T. Miyamoto
1930	T. Miyamoto
1931	R. Asami
1932	T. Miyamoto
1933	K. Nakamura
1934	Not played
1935	T. Miyamoto
1936	T. Miyamoto
1937	Chin Sei Sui
1938	R. M. Fuku
1939	T. Toda
1940	T. Miyamoto
1941	En Toku Shun
1942–49	Not played
1950	Y. Hayashi
1951	Son Shi Kin
1952	T. Nakamura
1953	Son Shi Kin
1954	Y. Hayashi
1955	K. Ono
1956	T. Nakamura
1957	H. Kobari
1958	T. Nakamura
1959	Chen Ching-Po
1960	H. Kobari
1961	K. Hosoishi
1962	T. Sugihara
1963	T. Toda
1964	H. Sugimoto
1965	T. Kitta
1966	S. Sato
1967	T. Kitta
1968	T. Kono
1969	H. Sugimoto
1970	M. Kitta
1971	Y. Fujii
1972	Hahn Chang Sang

1973	B. Arda
1974	M. Ozaki

New Zealand Open

Year	Winner
1907	A. D. S. Duncan
1908	J. A. Clements
1909	J. A. Clements
1910	A. D. S. Duncan
1911	A. D. S. Duncan
1912	J. A. Clements
1913	E. S. Douglas
1914	E. S. Douglas
1915–18	Not played
1919	E. S. Douglas
1920	J. H. Kirkwood
1921	E. S. Douglas
1922	A. Brooks
1923	A. Brooks
1924	E. J. Moss
1925	E. M. Macfarlane
1926	A. J. Shaw
1927	E. J. Moss
1928	S. Morpeth
1929	A. J. Shaw
1930	A. J. Shaw
1931	A. J. Shaw
1932	A. J. Shaw
1933	E. J. Moss
1934	A. J. Shaw
1935	A. Murray
1936	A. J. Shaw
1937	J. P. Hornabrook
1938	A. D. Locke
1939	J. P. Hornabrook
1940–45	Not played
1946	R. H. Glading
1947	R. H. Glading
1948	A. Murray
1949	James Galloway
1950	Peter W. Thomson
1951	Peter W. Thomson
1952	A. Murray
1953	Peter W. Thomson
1954	R. J. Charles
1955	Peter W. Thomson
1956	K. W. Berwick
1957	K. D. G. Nagle
1958	K. D. G. Nagle
1959	Peter W. Thomson
1960	Peter W. Thomson
1961	Peter W. Thomson
1962	K. D. G. Nagle
1963	B. W. Devlin
1964	K. D. G. Nagle
1965	Peter W. Thomson
1966	R. J. Charles
1967	K. D. G. Nagle
1968	K. D. G. Nagle
1969	K. D. G. Nagle
1970	R. J. Charles
1971	Peter W. Thomson
1972	W. Dunk
1973	R. J. Charles

1974	R. Gilder

Portuguese Open

Year	Winner
1953	E. C. Brown
1954	A. Miguel
1955	F. Van Donck
1956	A. Miguel
1957	Not played
1958	P. Alliss
1959	S. Miguel
1960	K. Bousfield
1961	K. Bousfield
1962	A. Angelini
1963	R. Sota
1964	A. Miguel
1965	Not played
1966	A. Angelini
1967	A. Gallardo
1968	Max Faulkner
1969	B. Hunt
1970	R. Sota
1971	L. Platts
1972	G. Garrido
1973	J. Benito
1974	B. Huggett

South African Open

Year	Winner
1905	A. G. Gray
1906	A. G. Gray
1907	L. B. Waters
1908	G. Fotheringham
1909	J. Fotheringham
1910	G. Fotheringham
1911	G. Fotheringham
1912	G. Fotheringham
1913	J. A. W. Prentice
1914	G. Fotheringham
1915–18	Not played
1919	H. G. Stewart
1920	L. B. Waters
1921	J. Brews
1922	F. Jangle
1923	J. Brews
1924	B. H. Elkin
1925	S. F. Brews
1926	J. Brews
1927	S. F. Brews
1928	J. Brews
1929	A. Tosh
1930	S. F. Brews
1931	S. F. Brews
1932	C. McIlvenny
1933	S. F. Brews
1934	S. F. Brews
1935	A. D. Locke
1936	C. E. Olander
1937	A. D. Locke
1938	A. D. Locke
1939	A. D. Locke
1940	A. D. Locke
1941–45	Not played
1946	A. D. Locke

1947	R. W. Glennie	1951	M. Provencio	1970	Graham Marsh
1948	M. Janks	1952	Max Faulkner	1971	Peter Townsend
1949	S. F. Brews	1953	Max Faulkner	1972	Graham Marsh
1950	A. D. Locke	1954	S. Miguel	1973	H. Baiocchi
1951	A. D. Locke	1955	H. de Lamaze	1974	R. J. Charles
1952	S. F. Brews	1956	P. Alliss		
1953	J. R. Boyd	1957	Max Faulkner		
1954	R. C. Taylor	1958	P. Alliss		
1955	A. D. Locke	1959	Peter W. Thomson		
1956	Gary Player	1960	S. Miguel		
1957	H. R. Henning	1961	A. Miguel		
1958	A. A. Stewart	1963	R. Sota		
1959	D. J. Hutchinson	1964	A. Miguel		
1960	Gary Player	1965	A. M. Gutierrez		
1961	R. Waltman	1966	R. DeVicenzo		
1962	H. R. Henning	1967	S. Miguel		
1963	R. Waltman	1968	R. Shaw		
1964	Alan Henning	1969	J. Garaialde		
1965	Gary Player	1970	A. Gallardo		
1966	Gary Player	1971	Dale Hayes		
1967	Gary Player	1972	A. Garrido		
1968	Gary Player	1973	N. Coles		
1969	Gary Player	1974	J. Heard		
1970	T. Horton				
1971	Simon Hobday				
1972	Gary Player				
1973	R. J. Charles				
1974	Bobby Cole				

Spanish Open

Swiss Open

Acknowledgements

Spanish Open		Swiss Open	
Year	Winner	Year	Winner
1912	A. Massy	1923	Alex Ross
1913–15	Not played	1924	Percy Boomer
1916	A. de la Torre	1925	Alex Ross
1917	A. de la Torre	1926	Alex Ross
1918	Not played	1927–28	Not played
1919	A. de la Torre	1929	A. Wilson
1920	Not played	1930	A. Boyer
1921	E. Laffitte	1931	M. Dallemagne
1922	Not played	1932–33	Not played
1923	A. de la Torre	1934	A. Boyer
1924	Not played	1935	A. Boyer
1925	A. de la Torre	1936	F. Francis
1926	F. Bernardino	1937	M. Dallemagne
1927	A. Massy	1938	J. Saubaber
1928	A. Massy	1939	F. Cavalo
1929	E. Laffitte	1940–47	Not played
1930	J. Bernardino	1948	U. Grappasonni
1931	Not played	1949	M. Dallemagne
1932	G. Gonzalez	1950	A. Casera
1933	G. Gonzalez	1951	E. C. Brown
1934	M. Provencio	1952	U. Grappasonni
1935	T. Cayarga	1953	F. Van Donck
1936–40	Not played	1954	A. D. Locke
1941	M. Provencio	1955	F. Van Donck
1942	G. Gonzalez	1956	D. J. Rees
1943	M. Provencio	1957	A. Angelini
1944	Luis I. Arana	1958	K. Bousfield
1945	C. Celles	1959	D. J. Rees
1946	M. Morcillo	1960	H. R. Henning
1947	M. Gonzalez	1961	K. D. G. Nagle
1948	M. Morcillo	1962	R. J. Charles
1949	M. Morcillo	1963	D. J. Rees
1950	A. Cerda	1964	H. R. Henning
		1965	H. R. Henning
		1966	A. Angelini
		1967	R. Vines
		1968	R. Bernardini
		1969	R. Bernardini

Action Photos by H W Neale 14, 81 (bottom), 124, 126, 127, 128 (left), 129, 131, 132 (bottom), 137, 140, 153 (top), 160 (top), 164, 165, 168, 169, 188 (top and bottom left), 194 (top right), 210, 219 (top)
Associated Press 57, 87, 89, 95, 96, 97 (top), 99, 100, 101, 102, 108, 111, 112, 114, 116-117, 118, 121, 123, 133, 135 (bottom), 141 (right), 184, 187 (top), 189, 202, 203, 216, 217, 218 (top)
The Bettman Archive 31, 103, 175
Bibliotheque Nationale 191
Camera Press 23 (bottom), 162 (bottom), 194 (top left)
Woodfin Camp/Marvin Newman 142 (top), 143
Colorsport Cover, title page, 144, 149, 151 (bottom), 154, 155 (bottom), 160 (bottom), 163, 166, 167 (top left and top right), 170
Henry Cotton 22 (top), 24 (bottom), 25 (bottom), 26 (top right and left), 45 (top), 50, 51, 71, 81 (top), 92, 97 (bottom), 106, 128 (right), 132 (top), 185, 186, 187 (bottom), 194 (top right), 197, 198 (bottom), 204, 205, 207, 209, 213 (left), 218 (bottom)
Gerry Cranham 138-139, 142 (bottom), 146, 150, 151 (top), 155 (top), 158, 159, 162 (top)
John Frost Collection 107
Frank Gardner 135 (top), 153 (bottom), 171, 172, 213 (right)
Sonia Halliday 11
Karquel 38-39
Keystone Press 161
E D Lacey 135 (top right), 148, 156 (top), 157, 188 (top right), 195
The Mansell Collection 33 (right), 35, 36-37, 40, 45 (bottom), 196
Presse Sports 156 (bottom)
Radio Times Hulton Picture Library 15 (top), 18-19, 20-21, 25 (top), 26 (bottom), 28, 29, 30, 33 (left), 42-43, 47, 48-49, 52, 53, 54 (top), 58, 59, 60-61, 63, 64, 66-67, 72-73, 74, 75, 76, 77, 78, 79, 80, 82-83, 84, 85 (bottom), 86, 88, 90, 91, 93, 94, 98, 104, 109, 176-177, 178, 180, 181, 183, 190, 192, 193, 200
Rijksmuseum 13, 16
Sport and General 44, 122, 141 (left)
Stedelijk Museum 17
Syndication International 65, 69, 73 (bottom), 147, 152, 167 (bottom), 215
USPGA 32, 46, 54 (bottom left and right), 115, 198 (top)
Roger Viollet 56, 85 (top), 174

Index